UNITED STATES

—■—v.—■—

NIXON

The Question
of Executive Privilege

GREAT SUPREME COURT DECISIONS

Brown v. Board of Education

Dred Scott v. Sandford

Engel v. Vitale

Furman v. Georgia

Gideon v. Wainwright

McCulloch v. Maryland

Marbury v. Madison

Miranda v. Arizona

Plessy v. Ferguson

Regents of the University of California v. Bakke

Roe v. Wade

United States v. Nixon

Great Supreme Court Decisions

UNITED STATES
— v. —
NIXON

The Question
of Executive Privilege

Larry A. Van Meter

CHELSEA HOUSE
PUBLISHERS
An imprint of Infobase Publishing

United States v. Nixon

Chelsea House
An imprint of Infobase Publishing
132 West 31st Street
New York, NY 10001

ISBN-10: 0-7910-9381-6
ISBN-13: 978-0-7910-9381-8

Library of Congress Cataloging-in-Publication Data
Van Meter, Larry A.
   United States v. Nixon : the question of executive privilege / Larry A. Van Meter.
      p. cm.
   Includes bibliographical references and index.
   ISBN 0-7910-9381-6 (hardcover)
   1. Executive privilege (Government information)—United States—Cases—Juvenile literature. 2. Nixon, Richard M. (Richard Milhous), 1913–1994—Trials, litigation, etc.—Juvenile literature. 3. Watergate Affair, 1972–1974. I. Title. II. Title: United States versus Nixon.
   KF4570.A7V36 2007
   342.73'06—dc22   2006023245

Chelsea House books are available at special discounts when purchased in bulk quantities for businesses, associations, institutions, or sales promotions. Please call our Special Sales Department in New York at (212) 967-8800 or (800) 322-8755.

You can find Chelsea House on the World Wide Web at http://www.chelseahouse.com

Text design by Erika K. Arroyo
Cover design by Takeshi Takahashi

Printed in the United States of America
Bang EJB 10 9 8 7 6 5 4 3 2 1

This book is printed on acid-free paper.

All links and Web addresses were checked and verified to be correct at the time of publication. Because of the dynamic nature of the Web, some addresses and links may have changed since publication and may no longer be valid.

Contents

1

The Plumbers

I n the early morning of June 17, 1972, as the faint sounds of automobile traffic echoed along the Potomac River, five burglars wearing business suits and rubber surgical gloves entered the Watergate Hotel in Washington, D.C. So they would not be seen, they had sneaked into the hotel from an underground garage. The Watergate, located on the banks of the Potomac, was one of the most luxurious hotels in town, home to many powerful and wealthy Washington politicians. Even at that time, rooms in the Watergate cost as much as $100,000 per year. Although the Watergate was primarily a Republican stronghold (it was the Washington residence of many powerful Republican figures[1]), it was also, curiously, the headquarters of the Democratic National Committee (DNC).

The U.S. presidential elections would be held a few months later. Current president Richard M. Nixon was a Republican. He had won a close election in 1968 and was just finishing his first term. It had been a rough presidency thus far: The nation had been mired in the Vietnam War for almost a decade. Nixon was concerned that the American people would seek different leadership in the November 1972 election, so he was trying to do everything in his power to ensure his victory.

In June 1972, however, Nixon did not yet have an opponent in the elections. The Democratic National Convention would not take place until the following month, but it was generally agreed that George McGovern, a senator from South Dakota, would win the Democratic nomination. McGovern was an outspoken critic of the Nixon presidency—most specifically of its handling of the Vietnam War—and Nixon's reelection officials feared that McGovern might pose a threat to Nixon's reelection campaign. As a result of that and other fears, an organization was set up to spy on the Democrats.

The five burglars sneaking along the corridors of the Watergate—James W. McCord, Bernard Barker, Virgilio Gonzalez, Eugenio Martinez, and Frank Sturgis—were trying to break into the Democratic National Committee office. These men were known as the Plumbers, part of a sophisticated and well-funded surveillance team. They were less sophisticated than believed, however, because at about 2:00 A.M., they were caught by a 24-year-old security guard, Frank Wills. As Wills was walking his regular rounds in the Watergate, he noticed that the door leading from the hotel's underground garage had been "taped:" Someone had put duct tape over the lock to keep the door from locking. Wills suspected that someone had picked the lock. Frightened and anxious that burglars might still be somewhere in the building, he quickly called the police. When the police arrived minutes later, they found that

Housed in the Watergate Hotel complex *(above)* in Washington, D.C., the Democratic National Party headquarters was burglarized on June 17, 1972. The seemingly minor event led to one of the United States' greatest government scandals.

the door to the DNC office had been completely removed. The Plumbers had failed to pick the DNC door lock, so they had taken the door off its hinges. In the now-open DNC office, the police discovered four men attempting to hide. (The fifth man, found in a different section of the hotel, was acting as a lookout.) One of the men in the office held a walkie-talkie, and, just as the police entered, he whispered into it, saying, "They got us."[2]

NO ORDINARY CRIMINALS

As they arrested the five men, the police found the following items in their possession: "40 rolls of unexposed film, two 35-millimeter cameras, lock picks, pen-size tear-gas guns, and bugging devices that apparently were capable of picking up both telephone and room conversations."[3] In addition, the burglars had more than $2,000 in cash, most of it in crisp, new, $100 bills. Finally, police found a notebook, with a cryptic message written in it: "E. Hunt W.H." When asked their identities, the perpetrators gave false names. The men were arrested and taken to the city jail. It was clear to the police that these were no ordinary criminals.

A few hours later, in front of Judge James A. Belsen, the men gave their real names. Several reporters were in the courtroom at the time. They were curious as to why five business suit–clad men would want to break into the Democrats' headquarters. The reporters also wondered why the men already had an attorney, a man named Joseph Rafferty, even though it was just a few hours since their arrest and none of the men had made a phone call from the jail.

When Judge Belsen asked the burglars about their profession, they answered that they were "anti-Communists." The man who appeared to be the leader of the group, McCord, added that he was a security consultant for the Central Intelligence Agency (CIA), a government agency that monitors the activities of other nations. Judge Belsen was startled, and a murmur spread through the courtroom. Why would someone working for the CIA be involved in a seemingly routine robbery? The answer, of course, was that there was nothing routine about the Watergate break-in.

In addition, the five men were not working alone. About three weeks earlier, on the night of May 28, 1972, the Plumbers had broken into the Democratic National Headquarters and planted two surveillance devices—telephone taps—on the phones of Lawrence O'Brien, chairman of the Democratic Party, and of Spencer Oliver, another high-ranking Democratic Party official.[4] The burglars had set up their espionage operation, which they called "Operation Gemstone," in a room at the Howard Johnson Hotel, across the street from

DEMOCRATS AND REPUBLICANS

For 150 years, there have been two dominant groups—known as parties—in the American political system: the Republican Party and the Democratic Party. Though it would be inaccurate and unfair to classify all Democrats or Republicans as uniform or inflexible in their political thinking, generally speaking, Republicans tend to be "conservative" and Democrats tend to be "liberal." Republicans, especially since the end of World War II, tend to believe in less government control over private and corporate affairs (a philosophy called *laissez-faire**); while Democrats tend to believe in active government and progressive social change. Since World War II, there have been six Republican presidents and six Democratic presidents:

YEARS	NAME	PARTY AFFILIATION
1932–1945	Franklin D. Roosevelt	Democratic
1945–1953	Harry S. Truman	Democratic
1953–1961	Dwight D. Eisenhower	Republican
1961–1963	John F. Kennedy	Democratic
1963–1969	Lyndon B. Johnson	Democratic
1969–1974	Richard M. Nixon	Republican
1974–1977	Gerald R. Ford	Republican
1977–1981	Jimmy Carter	Democratic
1981–1989	Ronald Reagan	Republican
1989–1993	George H.W. Bush	Republican
1993–2001	William J. Clinton	Democratic
2001–	George W. Bush	Republican

* *Laissez-faire* is a French term that means "to leave alone."

the Watergate. After a short time, however, those devices had malfunctioned. So the Plumbers had broken in on June 17 to repair the broken devices. As McCord, Barker, Gonzalez, Martinez, and Sturgis attempted to replace the "bugs," the architects of "Operation Gemstone," G. Gordon Liddy and E. Howard Hunt, were anxiously waiting in the Howard Johnson hotel room.

THE ARCHITECTS

E. Howard Hunt was born in 1918 in Hamburg, New York. During World War II, he worked for the U.S. Navy, the Army Air Corps, and the Office of Special Services (OSS), the forerunner to the Central Intelligence Agency. Hunt was also the author of pulp spy novels, writing more than 40 books, most of them under pseudonyms.[5] In 1949, he began his career as a CIA operative. Brash and confident, Hunt introduced himself to Richard Nixon in the 1950s, when Nixon was vice president to Dwight Eisenhower. In a Washington restaurant, Hunt had boldly walked up to Nixon's table and told Nixon that he was a great admirer of his. Nixon was flattered and invited Hunt to finish dinner at his table. Remembering the CIA agent a few years later, Nixon consulted Hunt in the failed U.S. efforts to overthrow Fidel Castro in Cuba.

In early 1970, Charles Colson, who worked as special counsel to President Nixon, wanted someone to head up a secret intelligence network, to be called the Special Investigations Unit (SIU), to spy on people the president did not trust. To Colson, Hunt seemed the perfect choice to lead the Special Investigations Unit: He had what Colson called "a cloak-and-dagger orientation."[6] Hunt's official job title was "consultant," but his real job was working as the top Plumber. Hunt was the man who had assembled the five-man insertion team of Plumbers, four of whom (Barker, Sturgis, Martinez, and Gonzalez) had worked with him during his anti-Castro activities. In the recovered

G. Gordon Liddy (*left*), one of the defendants in the Watergate Trial, leaves the District Court in Washington, D.C., on January 29, 1973. Liddy was the chief operative for Nixon's Plumbers and orchestrated the Watergate burglary.

Plumbers' notebook, the "E. Hunt" stood for E. Howard Hunt. The "W.H." stood for "White House."

The seventh member of the team was Hunt's copartner, G. Gordon Liddy. Born in 1930 in Hoboken, New Jersey, the son of an attorney, Liddy was educated at Fordham University in New York. In the 1950s and 1960s, Liddy worked as an FBI (Federal Bureau of Investigations) agent, but in 1971 he landed his dream job. John Mitchell, who was at that time attorney general of the United States, recruited Liddy to work with Hunt in the Special Investigations Unit.

Liddy's official job title was "legal adviser" for a pro-Nixon organization called "The Committee to Reelect the President" (CRP). The CRP job, however, was a front; that is, his real job was working side-by-side with Hunt in the Special Investigations Unit. The SIU received its financing through the CRP. According to historian Anthony Lukas, "[L]egal talent wasn't really what [the CRP] was looking for and it was almost certainly Liddy's FBI and Plumber experience which got him his job."[7] Though Hunt and Liddy had worked together on a few assignments before 1972, their top priority during the election year was Operation Gemstone. Like his partner Hunt, Liddy was a dangerous man, obsessed with guns, violence, and espionage.

The man on the other end of the walkie-talkie conversation during the night of the break-in was Howard Hunt. As soon as he heard "They got us," he and Liddy sprang into action. Hunt remembered that one of the Plumbers, Barker, had a key to the Howard Johnson hotel room (the key had both the hotel name and the room number etched onto it), so he and Liddy worked feverishly to remove all the evidence: "Hunt and Liddy began throwing McCord's surplus electronic gear and other 'operational litter' into suitcases. The long automobile antenna they had used to give their walkie-talkie extra range wouldn't fit into any of their bags, so Hunt thrust it

Evidence from the Watergate break-in is held in the U.S. National Archives. This phone book belonged to burglar Bernard Barker and was used to link the burglars' connection to Nixon's White House. The initials "HH" on the right-hand page refer to Howard Hunt, a consultant for Nixon's "Special Investigations Unit."

down one of his pants legs [. . . .] They jumped into a car and drove away."[8]

From the Howard Johnson Hotel, Hunt dropped Liddy off at his car, which was parked a few blocks away, then raced to his third floor office in the Executive Building (located on Pennsylvania Avenue, just a short distance from the White House). He dumped the suitcases filled with electronic equipment in the office and opened up his safe, taking out $10,000 in cash. He then called an attorney, C. Douglas Caddy, telling him there was an emergency. Hunt drove to Caddy's apartment and handed over $8,500 in cash, instructing Caddy to bail out the Plumbers. Caddy called Joseph Rafferty, who drove to the Metropolitan Police Headquarters the next morning to represent the five men.

MUCH MORE THAN A BURGLARY

Police had, in actuality, found two Howard Johnson room keys in the Plumbers' possession. One was to Room 214, one to 314. The police acquired a search warrant and entered the rooms the following afternoon. In their haste to remove evidence, Hunt and Liddy had nevertheless left many things behind: "[Police] found some more electronic equipment, more surgical gloves, several suitcases, and $3,566.58 in cash ($3,200 was in sequentially numbered $100 bills)."[9] It all seemed very strange and suspicious.

Little did anyone know at the time that this botched robbery attempt would turn out to be one of the most infamous events of twentieth-century American history. When investigators began looking into the background of the burglars—where they were from, for whom they were working, and why they were trying to break into the DNC—shocking realities emerged. As police, FBI, and media investigators began to piece together the puzzle of the Watergate break-in, it became clear that the burglars had connections that went all the way up to the highest official in America, the president of the United States. As Richard Ben-Veniste and George Frampton explained in their book *Stonewall*, the Watergate break-in and subsequent cover-up was the most high-reaching conspiracy to obstruct justice in history—a concerted effort by the most powerful men in government, including the president, to cover up the facts behind the break-in and to sidetrack the criminal investigation conducted by the United States Attorney's office and the Federal Bureau of Investigation.[10]

President Richard Nixon, implicated in the break-in and subsequent cover-up, would assert that he was immune from the consequences of the investigation. He claimed "executive privilege," that is, that the president of the United States was outside the jurisdiction of federal law. Ultimately, the Watergate scandal would draw the attention of the United States Supreme Court, whose interest in the case centered on this issue of "executive privilege." In short, it was a showdown between two powerful branches of American government. At no time in American history had a president so dramatically asserted his privilege or so dramatically challenged the power of the Supreme Court.

2

Break-in and Cover-Up

O ne of a plumber's jobs is to plug leaks. The two Plumbers not arrested in the bungled Watergate break-in, Howard Hunt and Gordon Liddy, were working feverishly to prevent information about the break-in from "leaking" to the American people. The Plumbers worked for the Special Investigations Unit, but it was a secret organization, so its financing was channeled through the Committee to Reelect the President. Hunt and McCord were "consultants" and Liddy a "legal adviser" for the CRP, but the other four were unofficially employed. As a result of their unofficial status, they could not receive normal employee wages. Instead they were paid in cash from a secret fund, called a "slush fund." Whenever the Special Investigations Unit was tasked with a secret job, it was given money from the slush fund, money that was located inside a safe at the offices of the CRP. Secret work tends to be very expensive (for example, the surveillance equipment seized by the police in the Watergate break-in was worth several thousand dollars), so there had to be a lot of money available to finance the work of the SIU. The CRP had hundreds of thousands of dollars available to finance their secret work. Where did that money come from? Who was in charge of it? Hunt and Liddy wanted to make sure that no one found out that information. They wanted desperately to cover their tracks so that, in the unlikely event of an investigation into the Watergate break-in, there would be no evidence available to investigators or media.

After arranging for an attorney for the arrested Plumbers, Hunt called James W. McCord's wife, instructing her to destroy all the surveillance equipment McCord kept at home. Liddy raced in his Jeep over to the Committee to Reelect the President headquarters and began shredding all documents related to Operation Gemstone.

NEWS SPREADS TO THE WEST COAST

At about 12:30 P.M. on June 17, Liddy put in a frantic call to the CRP's high-ranking officers, who had been attending a Republican Party function in Los Angeles, California. Liddy wanted to warn them that the Plumbers had been arrested and that, as a result, disaster could occur. Enjoying breakfast at the Polo Lounge in the Beverly Hills Hotel that morning were John Mitchell, chair of the CRP (and former attorney general of the United States); Jeb Magruder, deputy director of the CRP; Robert Mardian, assistant attorney general; Frederick LaRue, special adviser to Mitchell; and Herbert Porter, scheduling director for the CRP. Magruder was summoned to the house phone to take Liddy's call:

LIDDY: You've got to get to a secure phone.

MAGRUDER: A secure phone? I don't know where a secure phone is, Gordon.

LIDDY: There's one at a military base at El Segundo, about ten miles from your hotel.

MAGRUDER: I haven't got time to go to a military base. What's so important?

LIDDY: Our security chief was arrested in the Democratic headquarters in the Watergate last night.

MAGRUDER: What? Do you mean McCord?

LIDDY: That's right. Jim McCord.[11]

Liddy then assured Magruder that none of the arrested men would talk. Panic-stricken nevertheless, Magruder raced back to the breakfast table to tell Mitchell the news. The CRP officials didn't want anyone to find a link between the Plumbers and the CRP. Years afterward, Magruder would write, "At some point that Saturday morning I realized that this was not all hard-nosed politics, this was a crime that could destroy us all."[12] The men at the table in the Polo Lounge devised a quick strategy: The first thing to do was to try to arrange for McCord's release from the Washington jail. Magruder recalled later, "It did not seem beyond our capacities to get one man out of the D.C. jail."[13] The other four arrested Plumbers were Cubans living in Miami, Florida, so it was unlikely that investigators would be able to link them to the CRP. McCord, however, *could* be linked to the CRP.

THE INS AND OUTS OF THE CRP

John Mitchell was the CRP's top official. He had been close friends with President Nixon since 1963, when both were lawyers working in a New York law firm. When Nixon won the presidency in 1968, one of his first orders of business was to name Mitchell attorney general—the highest legal official in the United States. According to the historian Fred Emery, "Mitchell showed unwavering devotion to Nixon."[14]

The security coordinator of Nixon's Committee to Reelect the president, James W. McCord, was one of the first to be arrested in connection with the break-in at the Democratic National Committee headquarters at the Watergate complex. An electronics expert, McCord led the burglary.

When Nixon began his reelection campaign in 1971, he offered the job of campaign manager to Mitchell. When Mitchell accepted, the CRP was formed. Mitchell then resigned as attorney general.

The CRP ran two separate operations. The first was an overt operation, meaning that it managed Nixon's reelection campaign out in the open. It raised money for legitimate campaign functions—parties, rallies, and voter recruiting. One of those legitimate functions was the Republican Party gala that the CRP members were attending that weekend. It was an event called "Celebrities for Nixon," attended by high-profile Republicans in the entertainment industry: "a galaxy of Hollywood stars drawn by the aphrodisiac of power into the Nixon firmament: John Wayne, Zsa Zsa Gabor, Jack Benny, Terry Moore, John Gavin, and Charlton Heston."[15]

The Special Investigations Unit was another operation run by the CRP, but it was a covert—or secret—operation. Its job was to spy on people the president did not trust and to attempt to sabotage and disrupt the campaigns of rival politicians.

The Special Investigations Unit's covert operations were financed by the slush fund. Much of the money in the slush fund had come from legitimate donors to the president's re-election campaign. That money, however, was redistributed to the slush fund. How many of the top officials in the CRP knew about the fund? Did all the men sitting at the table in the Polo Lounge know about the slush fund? Did they all know about the Plumbers? Did they all know about the Plumbers' operations? These were important questions that would have to be answered sooner or later.

As chairman of the CRP, John Mitchell knew everything about the Special Investigations Unit's covert operations. After the break-in and subsequent arrest of the Plumbers, as was true for Liddy and Hunt, Mitchell was in a panic about the potential consequences if people were to find out that James McCord was involved in the CRP. So Mitchell sent instructions to Liddy to call the attorney general of the United States, Richard Kleindienst, so that Kleindienst could order McCord's immediate release from jail. Liddy drove out to a golf course in Washington, D.C., to meet with Kleindienst personally. Liddy told him the whole story, but Kleindienst was furious at the sloppiness of the operation and refused to order McCord's release. The important information to consider here, though, is that less than 24 hours after the arrest of the Plumbers, the attorney general knew about the incident. While Liddy was talking to Kleindienst, Judge Belsen set bail for the burglars at $30,000 for McCord and $50,000 for the four other men.

"OPERATION GEMSTONE" BEGINS TO UNRAVEL

Meanwhile, police and FBI investigations into the Watergate break-in were gathering steam. By late in the morning of June 17, FBI investigators had figured out two things: (1) that McCord, in addition to being a former CIA agent, was associated with the CRP, and (2) that the "E.H." code in the burglars' notebook was a reference to E. Howard Hunt. A special agent, Al Wong, was sent to Hunt's home to get some information, but Hunt said he would have to talk to his lawyer before he would talk to the police. After the FBI interview, Hunt went "underground," ultimately winding up hiding in California. The strategy had begun: Destroy all evidence and admit nothing.

The next day, June 18, 1972, the front page of the *Washington Post* ran a story on the Watergate break-in. Although it seemed strange that five men identifying themselves as anti-Communists would want to break into the Democratic National Committee headquarters, no reporters had yet made the connection between McCord and the CRP. That same day, the CRP team flew back from California to Washington; their job was to make sure that no one would make that connection.

After debarking from his plane in Washington, Jeb Magruder sped to the CRP headquarters to meet with a man named Hugh Sloan, the CRP treasurer. Magruder wanted to know whether the $100 bills found in the Plumbers' possession (money that had been removed from the CRP safe) could be traced to the CRP. In his book, *An American Life*, Magruder described that meeting: "Sloan was nervous when he came to my office, obviously very shaken, and his reply to my question left me shaken too. He said the money found on the burglars was money he had given to Liddy, and that it probably could be traced to us."[16]

OTHER PLUMBER OPERATIONS

Before being caught in the Watergate break-in, the Plumbers had performed two other major operations. The first was an attempt to discredit a man named Daniel Ellsberg. In 1971, Ellsberg had published *The Pentagon Papers*, a document that revealed alarming aspects of the United States' involvement in Vietnam. Enraged at Ellsberg, the Plumbers infiltrated Ellsberg's psychiatrist's office in Beverly Hills, California, during the Labor Day weekend in 1971 in order to dig up unflattering information that might discredit Ellsberg. Perhaps expecting something might happen, Ellsberg's psychiatrist, Dr. Lewis Fielding, had removed Ellsberg's files a few days earlier, thereby thwarting the Plumbers' plan*.

The second major operation was a sabotage of the Edmund Muskie presidential campaign. In February 1972, Muskie, a Democratic Senator from Maine, was running ahead of Nixon in early campaign polls. The Plumbers subsequently ran a "smear campaign," that is, they told lies, wrote fabricated letters to various newspapers, and spread false rumors in the areas where Muskie was campaigning. They even managed to get a CRP operative to get a job as Muskie's chauffeur. This sabotage was successful, as Muskie abandoned the campaign in April 1972**.

---

* See Liddy 157–169; and Lukas 97–102.
** See Emery 74–105.

The reason the money could be traced to the CRP, explained Sloan, was that a new law had recently (on April 7, 1972) gone into effect that prevented large cash donations from being made anonymously. Under the new law, donors' names would have to be listed. So before the new law had gone into effect, huge sums of last-minute cash donations had poured into the CRP treasury. According to Magruder, more than $6 million in cash was sent to the CRP in the two days preceding April 7. Twenty-five thousand dollars of that money had been in the form of a cashier's check from Minnesota. Sloan had given that check to Liddy, who cashed it in the form of sequentially numbered $100 bills. Some of those bills had been found on the arrested Plumbers. So, in other words, the money found on the Plumbers could possibly be traced directly to the CRP. For Magruder and the rest of the CRP committee, that was very bad news. If the president's men were to successfully stonewall any investigation into Watergate, they needed to cover tracks that might lead from the Plumbers to the CRP.

THE INVESTIGATION GAINS MOMENTUM

The investigative net was beginning to tighten, however. By the end of the weekend, FBI investigators had established that McCord had connections with the CRP. The chair of the Democratic National Committee, Lawrence O'Brien—who had been the target of Operation Gemstone—read the *Washington Post* article and demanded an immediate investigation, saying the break-in "raised the ugliest question about the integrity of the political process that I have encountered in a quarter century of political activity."[17] O'Brien knew that someone was trying to spy on him, but at such an early time in the investigation, he wasn't sure who. By the end of the day on Sunday, June 18, 1972, a huge story was starting to unfold. Little did most Americans know, however, just how huge a story it was to become.

On Monday, June 19, more of the major players in the Watergate crisis returned to Washington. The most significant was

President Nixon, who had spent the weekend at his summer home in Key Biscayne, Florida. During his helicopter flight, accompanied by his chief of staff, H.R. Haldeman, Nixon picked up a copy of a Florida newspaper, the *Miami Herald*, and saw a front-page headline that read, "MIAMIANS HELD IN D.C. TRY TO BUG DEMO HEADQUARTERS." In his memoirs, Nixon claimed that the *Miami Herald* headline was the first he heard of the Watergate break-in.[18]

At the president's request, Nixon's press secretary, Ron Ziegler, called a press conference to discuss the Watergate break-in, calling it a "third-rate burglary attempt" unworthy of further comment.[19] The CRP team, who 36 hours earlier had been rubbing elbows with Republican celebrities in Hollywood, were now in John Mitchell's Washington apartment (located, ironically enough, in the Watergate Hotel), devising a strategy on how to limit the amount of information that might leak. Mitchell instructed his CRP colleagues to destroy any evidence that might link them to the break-in.[20] Knowing that he had incriminating Gemstone evidence in his possession, Magruder asked Mitchell what he should do with it. Mitchell responded, "Maybe you ought to have a little fire at your house tonight."[21] Magruder left the meeting, drove to Bethesda, Maryland, to play three sets of tennis with Vice President Spiro Agnew, then went home to toss a five-inch-thick file of Operation Gemstone papers into his fireplace.

At the White House, John Ehrlichman, assistant to the president for domestic affairs, was "put in charge of containing the burgeoning scandal."[22] Ehrlichman's assistant in the Watergate damage control was to be John Dean, special counsel to the president. Dean, as it turns out, had been present at many planning sessions for Operation Gemstone. Ehrlichman's first instructions were to get Hunt and Liddy out of town, preferably even out of the country.

On the afternoon of June 19, despite Press Secretary Ron Ziegler's assurances that the break-in was an insignificant affair,

John N. Mitchell *(left)* served as campaign manager for his friend, Richard M. Nixon *(right)*. Once president, Nixon appointed Mitchell to the position of U.S. attorney general. Mitchell believed in law and order over civil liberties and was an advocate of wire tapping.

the United States Justice Department announced a full investigation into Watergate.

At 9:00 A.M. the following morning, in John Dean's office at the White House, Dean, Richard Kleindienst[23], H.R. Haldeman, John Ehrlichman, and John Mitchell—all high-ranking officials in the U.S. government—met to move into the next phase of the cover-up: "After three days of drift and improvisation, the President's men sought to regain control of the slippery situation."[24] They all agreed that the first order of business was to destroy all available evidence related to Operation Gemstone. They believed that, even though the Justice Department had begun an official investigation into the break-in, there still might be enough time to get rid of any evidence that might link the Plumbers to the White House.

The most important piece of evidence was a memorandum called "Memo 18." It was a document from Gordon Strachan[25] to Haldeman, written in April 1972. The memo authorized $300,000 of CRP money to be budgeted specifically for Special Investigations Unit operations. Haldeman ordered Strachan to destroy the document immediately, which he did. They also dispatched some men to CRP headquarters to open Howard Hunt's safe. In his safe were the following items:

- a .25 caliber pistol with ammunition and a holster;
- Frank McCord's briefcase, which contained tear gas, microphones, earphones, antennas, and wires;
- two cloth notebooks;
- an address book; and
- various folders and files containing secret information.

Dean asked Ehrlichman what they should do with the evidence. Ehrlichman told Dean to shred the documents and "deep six" the rest. Not knowing what "deep six" meant, Dean asked Ehrlichman to explain. Ehrlichman said, "You drive across the river on your way home at night, don't you? Well, when you cross over the bridge on your way home, just toss the briefcase into the river."[26] However, because several people—including a Secret Service agent—had witnessed the men remove the material from Hunt's safe, they instead decided to hand over the material to Patrick Gray, acting director of the FBI. Gray was loyal to President Nixon and would likely destroy any evidence if he were instructed to do so. At the very least, Gray could be counted on to stall any investigations into the break-in and cover-up.

Because investigators had already made the connection between McCord and the CRP, Lawrence O'Brien, chair of

The April 30, 1973, cover of *Time* magazine features a cartoon of Nixon and his top officials tangled in wire, a reference to the scandalous wire tapping conducted by the White House. Clockwise from top left are: James W. McCord, Jeb Magruder, H.R. Haldeman, John W. Dean, John Mitchell and Maurice Stans.

the Democratic National Committee, filed a one-million-dollar lawsuit against the CRP. The lawsuit was worrisome to the Republicans because once a lawsuit is filed, as Lukas explained in *Watergate*, the "legal discovery process" begins: "O'Brien's lawyers could now call as witnesses and take sworn depositions from almost the entire CRP and White House staffs."[27] In other words, if any evidence linking the Plumbers to the CRP remained, it could be "subpoenaed" (that is, ordered into a trial as evidence). Back at the White House, the president's men were trying to ensure that there wouldn't be any evidence.

THE COVER-UP PLAN IN THREE FORMS

On the following day, Wednesday, June 21, 1972, according to historian Fred Emery, "the cover-up suddenly moved to take on what would be its final shape."[28] Haldeman, Nixon's chief of staff, was nervous, wondering whether there was "something we can do other than just sitting here and watching it drop on us bit by bit."[29] The plan, devised by John Ehrlichman,[30] was in three forms. The first was to "stonewall," that is, to do nothing. Because the break-in seemed so bungled and amateurish, the president's men figured no one would suspect that the top officials in the U.S. government *could* be involved. In a meeting with John Dean, President Nixon said, "I'm not going to worry about it [. . .] At times, uh, I just stonewall it."[31] The second form, should investigators make the connection between the Plumbers and the CRP, was to blame the whole crime on Gordon Liddy. Emery wrote:

> The Ehrlichman scenario Haldeman unveiled to the President was something they knew to be made of whole cloth. It was that Liddy had pulled off Watergate as his own idea. Liddy would confess, saying "I thought it would be a good move, it would build me up" in CRP operations. Haldeman says of Liddy that "apparently he is a little bit nuts" . . . the beauty of the Liddy scenario is that all the guys think he is

I think we may very well be confronted with a dilemma that goes about like this: The President should be re-elected because he is making enormous strides in assuring this country's national security as a result of all of the accomplishments vis a vis other nations. If he had four more years he could do enormously important things to ensure long-range peace.

Yet, proficiency and accomplishment on the national security side is not respectable these days in the eyes of the media. It is unrespectable in the same sense that the military-industrial complex, the defense budget, the B-1, and now the F-14 are all being made suspect.

True but?

Our political enemies are opposing us vigorously on the national security side and pressing their strength on domestic issues. It seems to me there's a chance here to use their strength against them by involving the President in some of those domestic issues as to which people are preconditioned by the media. The environment is respectable according to the media, for example. *What else? Do you mean the real issues like economy & drugs — n The phonies like health & environment?* I have not answered your request for an analysis of the strong points to be emphasized and the issues to be pressed. I thought I would like to wait until after the budget meetings next week to do this.

How?

This 1973 memo written by John Ehrlichman to H.K. Haldeman mentions "political enemies." The comments in red are Haldeman's.

the top guy. Once the story was out the Nixon campaign would "ask for compassion"—[Liddy] is a poor misguided kid who read too many comic books.[32]

The third form was to pay off all people associated with the break-in to make sure they never talked. These payments were to be called "hush money."

Understanding the ramifications of the Watergate affair, John Dean, chief counsel to President Nixon, then seized control of the Watergate cover-up.[33] In his memoir of Watergate, *Blind Ambition*, Dean said that the president's men knew that, should a careful investigation of the break-in take place, "the vulnerability went right into the President's office."[34] Dean called Patrick Gray, acting director of the FBI,[35] to instruct him to stonewall any investigations into the Watergate affair. Dean wrote, "[W]e felt we could count on Pat Gray to keep the Hunt material from becoming public, and he did not disappoint us."[36]

The following day, June 22, 1972, while John Dean was trying to raise hush money to silence the perpetrators of the Watergate break-in, President Nixon called a press conference to comment on the recent events: "As Mr. Ziegler has stated, the White House has had no involvement whatever in this particular incident. As far as the matter now is concerned, it is under investigation, as it should be by the proper legal authorities, by the District of Columbia police, and by the FBI."[37]

Denial. Stonewall. Hush money. Deceit. These were the post-Watergate practices of some of the most powerful men in American government. How far were the president's men willing to go, however, to ensure that the American people would not find out the truth about the Watergate break-in?

One of the most interesting questions that have come up in the three decades since Watergate is: Why didn't the White House just confess that it was involved in the break-in, ask for forgiveness from the American people, and move on? One of the things President Nixon stressed in his private conversations during that time was that everybody seemed to be spying on everybody else. The United States was spying on the Soviet Union. The Soviet Union was spying on the United States. The CIA was spying on the FBI, the FBI on the CIA. The Republicans were spying on the Democrats, and vice versa. It was quite likely that the American people would have been upset to learn that agents hired by the Committee to Reelect the President were spying on the Democrats, but they probably would have, after a time, forgiven and forgotten. The president's men did not play it that way, though—they preferred to keep Watergate secret. And one thing is for certain: Once the ball was rolling in the White House plan to sabotage investigations into the affair, it was too late to change plans.

EQUAL·JUSTICE·UNDER·LAW·

3

Cover and Undercover

Although the acting director of the FBI, Patrick Gray, seemed like he would cooperate with the plan to stonewall the Watergate investigation, he operated by the book. In his book *Nightmare: The Underside of the Nixon Years*, Anthony Lukas wrote, "At the start, before he realized the depth of the White House involvement in the Watergate affair, Gray and his agents performed conscientiously."[38] As a matter of fact, they had traced the $100 bills found in the possession of the Watergate burglars to a bank in Miami, Florida, so "it was only a matter of time before they traced them back to the finance arm of the Committee to Reelect the President."[39]

On Thursday, June 23, 1972—not yet one week since the break-in—H.R. Haldeman met with President Nixon to discuss the White House strategy to limit the fallout regarding Watergate. Like Dean, Haldeman was worried about a potential FBI investigation into the affair. Things had been predictable during J. Edgar Hoover's half-century term as FBI director, but Hoover had died fewer than two months prior to the break-in. The president's men were concerned about what might happen if the FBI got involved. As they sat together, drinking coffee in the oval office, Haldeman said:

> Now, on the investigation, you know the Democratic break-in thing [the Watergate break-in], we're back in the problem area because the FBI is not under control, because [Patrick] Gray doesn't exactly know how to control it and they have, their investigation is now leading into some productive areas because they haven't been able to trace the money . . . and it goes in some directions we don't want it to go.[40]

A call was put in to Gray: Stall the investigation. To no one's surprise, Gray obeyed. According to Fred Emery in his book *Watergate*, Gray stalled the investigation "for another ten to fourteen days. By that time, the heat was off, and the cover-up well and truly launched."[41]

Gray's willingness to stall the investigation, however, did not stop the wheels of justice from turning. That same day, Thursday, just a few blocks away from the White House, a Federal Grand Jury had been put together to investigate the five men who had been arrested in the Watergate break-in— ironically, the same day McCord and the other four arrested Plumbers were released on bail. McCord was immediately fired as an employee of the CRP. The bail money, like the money used to finance the Special Investigations Unit, had come from the CRP. For a few days, things remained calm. It appeared for a moment that the White House strategy to cover up the Watergate break-in had been successful.

Soon things started to unravel, however. One of the biggest problems was the conscience of the CRP treasurer, Hugh Sloan. Sloan had authorized $199,000 in payments to Gordon Liddy. That huge sum would have been challenging to explain to a potential investigator. According to Lukas, "It would be very difficult to show that Liddy had been given $199,000 for purely legal purposes; $40,000, yes; $80,000, perhaps; but $199,000! Panic began to set in at CREEP." [42]

Magruder called in Sloan for a meeting. In his memoir, Magruder recalled their conversation:

> "Hugh, you may have a problem," I said. "You may have to find some other way to explain that money."
>
> "Do you mean commit perjury?"
>
> "You might have to."
>
> Sloan shook his head and departed, a very despondent young man, and one who was to be the source of many problems to us and many leaks to the newspapers. [43]

The inner circle of the president's men—Haldeman, Ehrlichman, Dean, Mitchell, Magruder, Gray—could all be counted on to protect the cover-up. Sloan, though, might crack under pressure.

A SPIRALING OF EVENTS

As many historians have noted, most of the actual law-breaking surrounding the Watergate break-in had already been committed by the end of June 1972: most specifically, the Plumber operations and the illegal channeling of campaign money. The more serious crimes related to the break-in began, however, once the burglars had been arrested. At that point, the CRP and the inner circle of presidential advisers began their campaign to contain information related to Watergate, to stall investigations on the break-in, to pay off potential witnesses in the case, and to deny any involvement. There were several

The accused men of the "Watergate seven" walk to their trial in Washington, D.C., on January 8, 1973. Shown arriving *(left to right)*: Virgilio Gonzales; Henry Rothblatt, attorney; Bernard Baker; Frank Sturgis; and Eugenio Martinez.

problems associated with their desire to conceal the crime, though: (1) There were too many people. (2) There were too many reporters sniffing around for information. (3) Pat Gray could only do so much to stall the FBI investigation. (4) The wheels of justice were turning too quickly for the president's men to stop them.

Once the Federal Grand Jury began its hearings on the Watergate break-in in late June 1972, things began to spiral out of control. The following is a timeline of key events:

- **June 28:** Liddy is fired as an employee of the CRP.
- **June 30:** Mitchell resigns as director of the CRP;

Clark MacGregor is named as his replacement.

- **July 1:** The FBI announces a nationwide manhunt for Howard Hunt.

- **July 12:** George McGovern is nominated as the Democratic candidate for president.

- **July 14:** Sloan resigns as treasurer of the CRP.

- **July 20:** Magruder testifies to the FBI that all money paid to Liddy was for legitimate intelligence operations.

- **July 28** Maurice Stans, chairman of the finance committee for the CRP, is subpoenaed to appear before the Grand Jury.

- **August 2:** At the request of Richard Kleindienst, attorney general of the United States, Stans is questioned by the U.S. Department of Justice rather than by the Grand Jury.

- **August 10:** Before the Grand Jury, MacGregor publicly names Liddy as the man who had transferred the famous $25,000 check from Minnesota into cash. This is the first public statement that campaign funds had been used to finance the Watergate break-in.

- **August 18:** Magruder commits perjury by telling the Grand Jury that all the money given to Liddy was for legitimate intelligence operations.

- **August 23:** Richard Nixon is nominated as the Republican candidate for president.

- **August 25:** Texas Congressman Wright Patman demands a congressional investigation into the CRP's use of campaign finances.

- **August 26:** The Government Accounting Office releases a report that the CRP had made 11 "apparent and possible violations" of the Federal Election Campaign Act.

- **August 28:** Kleindienst announces that the Justice Department will conduct a thorough investigation into the Watergate affair.

- **August 29:** President Nixon calls a press conference and announces that "no one in the White House staff, no one in this Administration, presently employed, was involved in this very bizarre incident."

- **September 2:** Mitchell informs reporters that he is "no way involved" and had "no advance knowledge" of the Watergate break-in.

- **September 9:** The Justice Department reveals that no one in the White House or the CRP staff is implicated in the Watergate investigation.

- **September 15:** The Grand Jury hands down indictments of the five men arrested in the Watergate burglary; it also indicts Hunt and Liddy. The Grand Jury announces, however, that "We have absolutely no evidence to indicate that any others should be charged."

HUSH MONEY

During this time period, the president's men were busy performing their cover-up operation. In his memoir, John Dean, the cover-up's "point man," wrote, "The cover-up blistered on, with me throwing water on it."[44]

One of the most important elements of the cover-up—other than the fact that the perpetrators remained quiet about the whole operation—was the reality of having to secretly raise money in order to pay off any potential informants. Lukas said, "In the ancient tradition of clandestine operations, someone had evidently assured the burglars and their chiefs before the break-in

DEEP THROAT

One of the great mysteries of Watergate was the identity of man whose code name was "Deep Throat." When *Washington Post* reporters Carl Bernstein and Bob Woodward began to piece together the Watergate conspiracy, they were receiving reports from an anonymous informant. Bernstein and Woodward's editor at the *Post*, Howard Simons, gave the informant the code-name "Deep Throat" because the reporters refused to reveal his identity. Bernstein and Woodward would use the information given to them by Deep Throat, but only if they promised not to reveal his identity. As a result, in their newspaper articles they would use his information, but refer to him only as "an unidentified source." As the Watergate cover-up began to unravel, it became clear to Bernstein and Woodward that Deep Throat was a very important man, a man who had access to much of the secret operations going on in the cover-up. In their famous book exposing the Watergate conspiracy, *All the President's Men*, they described Deep Throat as "a source in the Executive Branch who had access to information at CREEP as well as the White House." The information provided by Deep Throat would prove crucial to uncovering the Watergate cover-up. Bernstein and Woodward promised never to reveal Deep Throat's identity until he gave them permission to do so. And they were true to their word: The identity of Deep Throat would remain a secret for more than 30 years, until, in 2005, Mark Felt, who was then 92 years old, finally came forward to admit that he was Deep Throat. Felt, who had joined the FBI in 1942, had risen to the rank of deputy director of the FBI during Pat Gray's tenure. Most information that went to Gray would cross Felt's desk first, so Felt was in a unique insider position with respect to the Watergate conspiracy.

that they would be 'taken care of' if they were caught."[45] Being "taken care of" meant that they would be paid to stay quiet.

For example, immediately after McCord was fired from the CRP, Martha Mitchell—John Mitchell's wife—called Magruder and said, "Why are you firing Jim McCord? Why are you throwing him to the wolves?"

Magruder assured her, "We'll do what we can for him."[46]

What they would do was pay him in secret. As Emery explained, "To keep the defendants quiet and willing to accept jail sentences, large cash sums were needed and promises of clemency [. . . .] The cash was to come from secret campaign donations."[47] Ultimately, the hush-money fund would reach one-half million dollars. Distributing the money might be difficult, though, so a "bag man" was hired, that is, a person who delivers secret payments.

The bag man in the cover-up operation was a man named Tony Ulasewicz, a former New York policeman who had been performing secret work for John Dean for several years. Ulasewicz, who adopted the code name "Mr. Rivers," delivered the cash payments in a hotel laundry bag, the cash in tight wads tied together with rubber bands. The first two payments of $25,000 each were to go to Douglas Caddy (the lawyer who showed up at the courthouse on June 20 to represent the arrested Plumbers) and William Bittman (Hunt's personal attorney). Caddy refused the payment; Bittman accepted the payment. Ulasewicz's primary job, though, was to pay off the Plumbers. Hunt, Liddy, McCord, and the other four Plumbers all had living expenses that needed to be paid, and those pay-offs came from a slush fund at the CRP. As such, the payments had to be delivered in secret. A five-month budget was devised:

> [The budget] included $3,000 a month in salary for Hunt, McCord, and Liddy; $700 a month "family support" for Barker, Martinez, Gonzalez, and Sturgis; a separate $23,000 for Barker, comprising $10,000 bail, $10,000 "under the

Former New York detective Anthony Ulasewicz *(right)* addresses the Senate Watergate Committee on July 18, 1973. Ulasewicz used pictures to show the various places he used as "hush money" drops to the Watergate defendants and their attorneys. Senator Daniel K. Inouye *(left)* and Senator Joseph M. Montoya *(center)* listen to the testimony.

table," and $3,000 for "other expenses"; $25,000 apiece to cover the legal fees of Hunt, McCord, Liddy, and Barker; $10,000 each for the other three defendants' legal fees, and $5,000 for Mrs. Hunt's personal expenses [. . . .] In all, the budget came to nearly $450,000.[48]

Frederick LaRue, who had served as Mitchell's adviser at the CRP, was placed in charge of transferring the money to Ulasewicz. LaRue would remove cash from the slush-fund safe at the CRP headquarters and deliver it in secret to Ulasewicz, who in turn would deliver it to the Plumbers.

In addition, Pat Gray was continuously stalling the FBI investigation, all the while informing John Dean of the investigation's status. Gray would often meet Dean in secret meetings, "during which [Gray] would hand [Dean] his personal attaché case filled with FBI reports."[49]

POOR TIMING FOR AN INVESTIGATION

One important element of the Grand Jury's investigation is that it occurred during the presidential election campaign. The president's men were very worried that the investigation might turn into a full-fledged scandal and hurt President Nixon's chances for reelection. "All this pales," Hunt wrote in a letter to a White House aide, "beside the overwhelming importance of re-electing the President and you may be confident that I will do all that is required of me toward that end."[50] For two months, the cover-up was working well. Dean explained, "As the cover-up progressed through July and August, I was struck by its tremendous political success. Secret White House polls indicated that the Watergate break-in had not made the slightest dent in the President's popularity."[51]

The Federal Grand Jury handed down its indictments on September 15, 1972. After more than two months of investigations, the Grand Jury returned an eight-count indictment against the five men (Bernard L. Barker, Frank S. Sturgis, Virgilio R. Gonzalez, Eugenio R. Martinez, and James W. McCord) arrested at the Democratic headquarters on June 17, plus Hunt and Liddy. The charges included tapping telephones, planting electronic surveillance devices, and theft of documents.[52] That day, John Dean had a conversation with President Nixon, saying, "I think that I can say that fifty-four days from now nothing will come crashing down to our surprise."[53]

The purpose of a Grand Jury, unlike a trial, is merely to establish whether there is enough evidence to warrant a trial. Thus the Federal Grand Jury investigating Watergate decided whether a case could be made against the seven men implicated in the break-in. Once the indictments were handed down, a trial would be scheduled.

On September 18, 1972, it was announced that the federal judge assigned to preside over the Watergate case, John J. Sirica, had scheduled the trial for November 15, 1972. The scheduled trial date was met with controversy: November 15 was *after* the presidential election—to be held on November 7—and many people wanted the trial to occur before the election, to determine whether high-ranking White House officials had been involved in the now-famous Watergate break-in. In his memoir, *To Set the Record Straight*, Sirica said, "[T]here was heavy pressure building to have the Watergate case tried before November, to get the facts out in the open before the American people cast their ballots in the Presidential election."[54] Before becoming a federal judge, Sirica had worked in various Republican organizations, most notably as a Republican delegate in the 1952 presidential election.[55] He was concerned that if the

DISTRICT COURTS

The indictments brought down in the Watergate Grand Jury demanded that the Plumbers be tried in a federal, rather than local or state, court. When drafting the United States Constitution, the Founding Fathers wanted to ensure that power be shared between the federal government and the various state governments (this concept is known as federalism). According to uscourts.gov, "The Founding Fathers of the nation considered an independent federal judiciary essential to ensure fairness and equal justice for all citizens of the United States." All states in the United States (and, in addition, the District of Columbia, Puerto Rico, Guam, the Virgin Islands, and the Northern Marian Islands) have district courts. The American district court system functions as a guarantee that local prejudices, passions, and biases do not prevent justice.

presiding judge in the Watergate case had Democratic Party ties, the decision might be perceived as politically motivated. As Sirica explained it, "[T]he important consideration was to have a fair trial, not a quick one."[56] On September 19, the seven indicted men pleaded not guilty to the charges against them. All during this time, Ulasewicz was continuing his secret cash payoffs.

With the Watergate trial on hold, the presidential election proceeded exactly as John Dean had predicted—an overwhelming victory for Richard Nixon. On Election Day, November 7, 1972, Nixon won in a landslide over George McGovern. If there was any voter anxiety about Watergate, it did not show at the polls. Nixon won "by a record margin of 49 states to one—and the lone McGovern win was not even his home state of South Dakota, but Massachusetts. Nixon's share of the vote, 60.7 percent, was just short of Lyndon Johnson's all-time record of 61.1 percent."[57]

The president's men's plan had worked: They had managed to cover up the Watergate conspiracy well enough to ensure Nixon's reelection. Now the election was over, though, and the more serious problems associated with Watergate were just beginning.

PROBLEMS PERSIST

The first problem to materialize concerned demands for more money from the Plumbers. Though the Plumbers were receiving secret cash payments from the CRP slush fund (LaRue to Ulasewicz to Plumber), some of the Plumbers were unhappy with the amounts they were receiving. Released on bail, an angry Howard Hunt called the White House on November 14, 1972, to complain about the payments. His call was directed to Charles Colson, special counsel to the president. As it turned out, Colson taped the phone conversation:

> HUNT: The reason I called you was . . . because of commitments that were made to all of us at the onset, have not been

kept. And there's a great deal of unease and concern on the part of the seven defendants [the Plumbers] and possibly, well I'm quite sure, me least of all. But there's a great deal of financial expense here that has not been covered and what we've been getting has been coming in dribs and drabs.[58]

Colson tried to calm Hunt down, promising him that within a few days more payments would be delivered. But Hunt was desperate and delivered a threat: "After all, we're protecting the guys who were really responsible [...] but at the same time, this is a two way street . . . and, as I've said before, we think that now is the time when some moves should be made and, uh, surely your cheapest commodity available is money."[59]

The threat, of course, is that if the Plumbers did not get paid, they would reveal the identity of "the guys who were really responsible." Frightened of the ramifications of Hunt's phone call, Colson sent the tape to John Dean. Dean wrote, "We both knew Hunt was a time bomb."[60] Dean then played the tape for Haldeman and Ehrlichman on November 15. Ehrlichman instructed Dean to play the tape to John Mitchell: "Why don't you have our friend John Mitchell take care of Mr. Hunt's problem? He's got a lot of free time up there in New York making money."[61] Dean then flew to New York to play the tape to Mitchell. Dean was hoping that Mitchell would perhaps promise more money to silence the increasingly nervous Hunt, but Mitchell merely listened to the tape and then left.

Hunt was not yet finished. Immediately after his conversation with Colson, Hunt wrote a 1,900-word memo to Kenneth Parkinson, a lawyer for the CRP. The memo threatened that the Plumbers would reveal their secrets if they were not paid in a timely fashion. Reminding Parkinson that "loyalty has always been a two-way street," Hunt's memo listed several demands that must be met, the most important being immunity from prosecution in the upcoming trial and more money. On November 20, Parkinson took the memo to

Ex-presidential aide Hugh Sloan (*right*) testifies at the Watergate hearings on June 1, 1973. Sloan was treasurer of Nixon's reelection committee but claimed to know nothing about the Watergate break-in. He was an important source for Carl Bernstein and Bob Woodward, the *Washington Post* reporters who investigated the scandal.

Dean. Dean wrote, "When the Hunt memo was passed to me I looked at it with dread. The money demands of each of the seven Watergate defendants were spelled out: salary, family up-keep, incidentals and lawyer fees."[62] According to Lukas, "[T]he White House recognized Hunt's memo as just what it was—a threat."[63] Several days later, Mitchell called Dean with a solution. Just before the Campaign Finance law went into effect in April 1972, another slush fund had been set up in the care of Haldeman. The amount in the fund was $350,000. According to Lukas, Mitchell "told Dean that to satisy the defendants' new demands he would have to use some of the $328,000 remaining in Haldeman's $350,000 secret fund."[64] Fifty-thousand dollars was immediately taken out of the fund and delivered to Bittman, Hunt's lawyer. The rest would be doled out to others associated with the break-in, perhaps most significantly to the family members of the Plumbers.

One final, tragic occurrence hastened the crumbling of the cover-up. On December 8, 1972, Dorothy Hunt, Howard Hunt's wife, was killed in a plane crash. On its approach to Chicago's Midway Airport, the Boeing 737 got lost in the fog and crashed into a neighborhood, killing 43 of the 55 passengers on board. Investigators sifting through the wreckage found in Mrs. Hunt's purse more than $10,000 in cash, mostly in sequentially numbered $100 bills. That cash had come from the CRP fund and possibly could be traced. Knowing that Mrs. Hunt was married to one of the Plumbers, Watergate investigators might grow suspicious about such a large sum of money in the possession of someone so closely related to the break-in. As a result of his wife's death, Howard Hunt changed his mind about pleading not guilty to the charges against him. Describing himself as a "broken man," Hunt didn't think he could handle the stress of a high-profile trial. He said, "I decided to plead guilty in hope that leniency would be accorded me."[65] The death of Dorothy Hunt signaled the beginning of a new phase in the Watergate crisis: From that point on, the cover-up would slowly and irreversibly deteriorate.

EQUAL·JUSTICE·UNDER·LAW·

4

Congress Intervenes

The original trial date for The Plumbers was set for November 15, 1972. Shortly before the trial was to begin, however, John Sirica, the presiding judge, injured his back and was forced to reschedule the trial for the beginning of the following year. The federal trial, *United States v. Liddy, et al.*, thus began on Wednesday, January 10, 1973. It was national news: Inside, the courtroom was packed, and outside were dozens of impatiently waiting news crews, all eager to hear what was going on in the famous trial. Judge Sirica described the courtroom scene:

> The defendants and their attorneys crowded around two
> tables to my right; the government prosecutors, [Earl]

Silbert, Seymour Glanzer, and Donald Campbell at a table to my left. Artists from the television networks, with their large sketch pads and colored pencils, crowded in among the scores of reporters gathered to hear the beginning of the trial of the seven Watergate defendants.[66]

The first phase of the trial is the opening statements. Each side in the trial—the prosecution and the defense—is allowed to make introductory comments. The first person to address the 12-person jury was Silbert, the chief prosecutor. The prosecution's job is to convict the accused, that is, to convince the jury that the accused is guilty of the crime—or crimes—brought against him or her. The prosecution in this particular case had to "prove" the eight indictments handed down by the Federal Grand Jury: "The first two counts charged Hunt and the others with conspiracy and with burglary. Counts 3, 4, 5, and 8 related to the bugging of the Watergate office. Hunt was not named in 6 and 7, which charged McCord and the Miamians with possessing illegal eavesdropping equipment."[67] The prosecution's job in this particular trial was even bigger than usual, however: Not only did the team need to convince the jury that the defendants had indeed committed the crimes they had been accused of, but, more important, it needed to establish the reasons for the crimes, and to determine whether other, higher-ranking people, were involved. In pretrial hearings in December 1972, Judge Sirica warned the prosecuting attorneys, "[The] jury is going to want to know somewhere down the line what did these men go into the headquarters for? What was their purpose? Who hired them to go in there? Who started this thing?"[68]

Silbert told the jury that Liddy had received a large amount of cash ($235,000) to perform intelligence operations against the Democratic Party, but that only a fraction of that money could be accounted for. Silbert said to the jury, "[T]he government doesn't have any records as to what happened to the rest of that money given to Mr. Liddy."[69] A more important

Artist Franklin McMahon's illustration of the Watergate arraignment shows a mass of attorneys gathered before Judge John Sirica.

question was left up to the jury, however: Was Liddy the Plumbers' boss? Was he acting independently, or were higher-ranking people involved?

Second to address the jury was the defense. There were four separate defense teams in the trial: one for McCord (Gerald Alch), one for the four Miamians (Henry Rothblatt), one for Hunt (William Bittman), and one for Liddy (Peter Maroulis). Alch and Rothblatt took their turns addressing the jury, each suggesting that their clients were merely taking orders from higher authorities (from Liddy? or perhaps from someone higher?).

When Alch and Rothblatt finished their opening statements, the trial took a dramatic turn. Expecting Bittman to echo the defense strategy of the two previous attorneys, the packed courtroom instead heard the shocking news that Hunt had changed his mind: "At this time, Your Honor," said Bittman to Judge Sirica, "Mr. Hunt wishes to withdraw his plea of not guilty." Gasps of surprise broke out in the courtroom. Everyone in the courtroom had fully expected Bittman to follow the example of the previous defense attorneys—to assert the innocence of the defendant. Hunt—who was not one of the five burglars caught red-handed in the DNC headquarters—was instead confessing his guilt! Perhaps stunned by the extraordinary turn of events, Judge Sirica recessed the proceedings, ordering that the trial resume the following day. Hunt's change of heart represented a profound change in the trial—and the court had not yet heard from Liddy, whom most people assumed to be in charge of the operation.

During the following two days, Thursday and Friday, another dramatic change occurred. The four Miamians— Barker, Sturgis, Gonzalez, and Martinez—changed their minds as well, and while the court proceedings were playing out, they tried to convince their attorney, Rothblatt, to follow Hunt's example and submit a guilty plea. Rothblatt, however, refused to reverse their not-guilty plea. According to Sirica, "Rothblatt was resisting the guilty plea because he felt his clients were be-ing pressured into following Hunt's example."[70]

Concerned that their attorney was not representing his cli-ents adequately, Sirica dismissed Rothblatt as the Miamians' lawyer and assigned a court-appointed attorney, Alvin Newmy-er, for the remainder of the case. When the court reconvened the following Monday, Newmyer, who had been convinced by the Miamians that they had not been coerced into changing their minds, reversed their original pleas and instead entered guilty pleas. Sirica was suspicious of the defendants' sudden change in heart: "I was determined that despite the pleas, I would make an attempt to find out what else they knew about the case."[71] The Miamians remained silent. Their silence had been purchased by the slush funds at the Committee to Reelect the President.[72]

THE TRIAL CARRIES ON

Two defendants still remained: Liddy and McCord. They did not follow the lead set by Hunt and the Miamians, though, and reasserted their not-guilty pleas. Meanwhile, the Miamians and Hunt were taken back into police custody. (Hunt was re-leased on $100,000 bail.) So, for the next two weeks, the trial progressed, the prosecution finally making its way toward the source of the Plumbers' money, the CRP. On Tuesday, January 23, Jeb Magruder, deputy director of the CRP, was called to the court to answer questions from the prosecution. Silbert wasted no time in getting to the key questions:

> Q. Mr. Magruder, did you ever give Mr. Liddy any assignment concerning the Democratic National Committee?
>
> A. No.
>
> Q. Did you ever receive a report of any kind from Mr. Liddy concerning the Democratic National Committee offices and headquarters?
>
> A. No.[73]

Magruder was calm and confident during the questioning, giving no indication that his testimony was perjury, a lie told in a court of law. Since the formation of the Special Investigations Unit, Magruder had been fully aware of its operations and also fully aware that those operations were being financed by slush funds at the CRP. Now, however, his denial of those facts was in the court record. It was a serious crime, but it would not come out for several months.

Next up on the witness stand was Hugh Sloan, the assistant treasurer for the CRP. Sloan told Silbert that yes, he had given money to Liddy, but that he did not know what that money was to be used for. Like Magruder's testimony, Sloan's was perjury as well. About Magruder's and Sloan's testimonies, Sirica said, "I just didn't believe these people. The whole case looked more and more like a big cover-up."[74] At that point, Judge Sirica dismissed the jury and began questioning Sloan one on one. Growing more and more suspicious about the payments to Liddy, Sirica wanted to know who had authorized the payments and whether anyone at the CRP knew why all that money was being paid out. Judge Sirica asked Sloan 42 questions about the CRP payments to Liddy. Sloan reasserted that higher officials had authorized those payments, and that he did not know what that money was to be used for. When questioned about the identity of those higher officials, Sloan named Jeb Magruder, John Mitchell, and Maurice Stans (treasurer of the CRP). The revealing of those significant names—especially the name of Mitchell, the former attorney general of the United States—would drive open a wedge in subsequent Watergate investigations. It was one of the first indications that higher-ranking officials than the Plumbers were involved in Watergate, a term that by the end of the year would be a household name.

To the frustration of both judge and jury, neither Liddy nor McCord would testify on his own behalf during the trial. Each "pleaded the fifth," that is, they invoked the Fifth Amendment to

DISBURSEMENTS
KALMBACH   250,000*
STRACHAN   350,000
PORTER   100,000*
LIDDY   199,000*
MAGRUDER   20,000
LANKLER   50,000
HITT   25,000
NOFZIGER   10,000*
STONE   15,000*
DOLE   3,000
OTHER   5,000*
                       _____
              TOTAL   1,777,000*

*approximation

Senator Joseph M. Montoya of New Mexico looks over testimony at the Watergate hearings as Hugh Sloan, Jr., testifies before the committee. The chart behind Montoya indicates the distribution of funds collected by the CRP.

the U.S. Constitution, which assures defendants in a U.S. court of law that they will not have to witness against themselves. Sirica said, "[T]here was apparently too much to lose in cross-examination by the government. They couldn't plead with the jury that [they] were being made scapegoats, since [they] were determined at that point to protect the higher-ups who had authorized the Liddy plan."[75]

The trial ended on January 30, 1973. The jury took one hour and 28 minutes to reach its verdict. To no one's surprise, Liddy and McCord were found guilty on all eight counts. Said Sirica, "There had never been any doubt about that result."[76] Sirica was also convinced that there was much more to the story, however. He suspected that Liddy had been set up as the "fall guy" in the Watergate break-in. (A fall guy is a person who takes all the blame for a crime when, in fact, there are more people involved.) In their testimony in the trial, Magruder and Sloan suggested that Liddy was running his spy operations unbeknown to CRP officials. Sirica thought that story to be too convenient and innocent; he simply did not believe it.

Sirica didn't know what the story was, though, so he delayed sentencing for the seven Plumbers for two months, scheduling it for March 23. What he hoped to determine during that time period was whether others had been involved in the break-in and whether forces were conspiring to silence the men on trial.

The federal trial, although not particularly revelatory, hastened the unraveling of the Watergate cover-up. In the following few weeks, the structure of the conspiracy would quickly destabilize and ultimately crumble. February and March 1973 would prove disastrous for the Watergate conspirators. As a result, the U.S. government would soon be in the midst of a crisis.

CONGRESS STEPS IN

On February 7, 1973, reacting to mounting pressures to get to the bottom of the Watergate controversy, the United States Congress entered the fray. By a margin of 70–0, the Senate voted to form a seven-member committee to investigate the Watergate break-in. Chairing the committee would be Senator Sam Ervin of North Carolina. The other committee members were Daniel K. Inouye of Hawaii, Joseph M. Montoya of New Mexico, Herman Talmadge of Georgia, Howard Baker of Tennessee, Edward Gurney of Florida, and Lowell Weicker, Jr., of Connecticut. Two days later, Nixon's inner circle of advisers—Ehrlichman, Haldeman, and Dean—flew to California to come up with a plan to deal with the impending Senate investigation. At the West Coast meeting, Dean was placed in charge of the White House plan to cover up its relationship with the Watergate break-in: "The White House will take a public posture of full cooperation but privately will attempt to restrain the investigation and make it as difficult as possible to get information and witnesses."[77] Because the Senate hearings would not formally begin for several weeks, the White House felt it had sufficient time to stonewall the Senate investigation.

On February 28, 1972, Pat Gray went before the U.S. Senate, who were trying to determine whether he was fit to be confirmed as permanent FBI director. At first, it looked as if Gray would be unanimously approved, one senator praising Gray as "a man of absolute integrity," another saying Gray would "perform his tasks on a completely nonpartisan basis."[78] During the hearings, however, Gray made an eye-opening admission:

> [W]ithout solicitation or undue prodding from the senators, he volunteered some startling new information about the Watergate matter: that as early as July, 1972 he had started turning data on the [FBI] investigation over to Dean, had discussed the progress of the inquiry on numerous occasions with Dean and Ehrlichman, and had allowed Dean to sit in on FBI interviews with Watergate figures.[79]

The senators were shocked. Why would the FBI reveal any information about a classified investigation, especially an

investigation that was still ongoing? Even more extraor-
dinarily, an investigation that might implicate people *in* the
White House? The senators then demanded that John Dean appear before them in the confirmation hearings. That demand
was met with panic at the White House. Fearing that too much
might come out regarding Watergate, President Nixon refused
to permit Dean to appear before the Senate. Citing "executive
privilege," Nixon said, "No President could ever agree to allow the counsel to the President [i.e., Dean] to go down and
testify before a committee."[80] In other words, Nixon believed
that the U.S. Constitution granted him the privilege to refuse to
appear—or allow his close advisers to appear—before a court
or congressional inquiry. It was this assertion of so-called executive privilege that would ultimately attract the attention of
the U.S. Supreme Court, although that court would not become
involved in the Watergate conspiracy for several months. The
Senate confirmation committee did not press the issue: They
withdrew their request for Dean's testimony and let the matter
drop. The matter of "executive privilege," however, would ultimately become a profoundly controversial issue.

SENTENCING AND SUSPICION

After the federal trial, Howard Hunt and James McCord anxiously awaited their sentencing and began to wilt under the
pressure. The president's men had arranged large cash payments to be made, to take care of the Plumbers (and their
families), but the payments were not always reliable. More
important, the Plumbers were worried about how long the
payments would last. They knew they were going to have to
spend time in prison, and they suspected that the cash payments might dry up once the prison terms began. Their only
bargaining chip was knowing that very powerful men were involved in the break-in and cover-up—that information might
prove more valuable than the irregular cash payments coming from the CRP slush funds. On March 16, Hunt (who was

CHECKS AND BALANCES

The U.S. government is divided into three separate branches—the executive, judicial, and legislative. The president occupies the executive branch, the Supreme Court constitutes the judicial branch, and Congress represents the legislative branch. As the authors of the Constitution imagined it, those three branches would be equal, moreover that those branches would function cooperatively as a system of "checks and balances." Congress passes laws, the president enforces those laws, and the Supreme Court interprets those laws. Though each branch of government has specific powers, those powers could be monitored and corrected (i.e., "checked") by the other branches. For example, Congress can pass a law, but the president can reject (or "veto") that law. Congress and the president can agree on a law, but the Supreme Court can reject the law as unconstitutional. This system is designed to ensure equality (i.e., "balance") among the three branches, to prevent any one branch of the government from having too much power. The system of checks and balances played a crucial role in Watergate. The Watergate crisis, perhaps more than any other single crisis in American governmental history, tested the limits of the checks and balances system. During Watergate, each branch of the government played a crucial role in asserting its power. Perhaps the most important question arising during the crisis was, what are the outer limits of executive power? When Nixon invoked "executive privilege" to prevent his officials from appearing before the Senate hearings, was he exercising too much power? Furthermore, did the other branches—specifically the judicial branch—have the power to "check" that exercise?

out of jail on a $100,000 bond) arranged a meeting with Paul O'Brien, a CRP lawyer, to discuss his financial needs. Hunt demanded $120,000 to cover legal fees and family support. (Hunt had four children.)[81] Hunt told O'Brien, "[I]f the White House was planning to abandon me, then I would have to consider my options."[82] Hunt did not say what these "options" might be, but it was clearly a threat that he might blow the lid off the cover-up if he weren't taken care of. O'Brien noted the demands and relayed them to John Dean, who interpreted the demands as blackmail: "Hunt was dragging me into his extortion loop. He must have learned that I was the one who had carried the money messages before, and now he figured he had a hold on me for more. I could see Hunt extorting me, milking me, for the rest of our lives."[83]

As he had done four months earlier, Dean contacted John Mitchell about Hunt's new set of demands. Although he was angry at the new demands, Mitchell nevertheless arranged for a cash payment of $75,000 to be delivered to Hunt's attorney, William Bittman. The delivery seemed like a scene from a spy movie: In the middle of the night on March 21, a "bag man," Manyon Millican, thrust a manila envelope stuffed with the money into Bittman's home mailbox. Alerted by an encoded telephone message, Bittman retrieved the cash at midnight, then immediately called Hunt to tell him that the payment had arrived. Hunt was very upset that there was far less money than what he had demanded. "I now realized," said Hunt, "I could count on no further assistance, financial or otherwise, from [. . .] Mitchell, Dean and Magruder."[84]

In a similarly desperate act, McCord had sent a letter to Judge Sirica, hinting that the Plumbers were merely pawns in a bigger game. Three days before the sentencing, on March 20, McCord delivered a letter to Sirica, who was surprised by the information in it:

1. There was political pressure applied to the defendants to plead guilty and remain silent.

2. Perjury occurred during the trial of matters highly material to the very structure, orientation, and impact of the government's case and to the motivation of and intent of the defendants.

3. Others involved in the Watergate operation were not identified during the trial when they could have been by those testifying.[85]

McCord's letter confirmed Sirica's suspicions that there was much more to the story than what had been revealed during the trial. Though McCord's letter did not name the "others involved" in the cover-up, it was now clear to Sirica that McCord "was refusing to go along with the cover-up."[86] More important, McCord's letter reinforced Sirica's suspicions that authorities higher than the seven men on trial were involved.

On sentencing day, Judge Sirica read McCord's letter aloud in the courtroom. Because of its extraordinary revelations, it was a very difficult letter for Sirica to read. As he read, "an excruciating pain began to build directly in the center of [his] chest."[87] Unable to continue the proceedings, Sirica announced a recess. According to Emery, "The courtroom erupted as reporters sprinted for the phones."[88] The American public must have had suspicions over the previous few months that the Plumbers had not been acting independently, and now those suspicions were coming closer to being confirmed.

After a one-hour rest, Judge Sirica regained his composure and recommenced the sentencing. Sirica said, "The Court has reached the opinion that the crimes committed by these defendants can only be described as sordid, despicable, and thoroughly reprehensible." He sentenced Liddy to serve a 20-year prison sentence and to pay a $40,000 fine.[89] Hunt was given a provisional 35-year sentence. Barker, Sturgis, Martinez, and Gonzalez were given provisional 40-year sentences.[90] Because

JAMES W. McCORD, JR.
7 WINDER COURT
ROCKVILLE, MARYLAND 20850

TO: JUDGE SIRICA   March 19, 1973

Certain questions have been posed to me from your honor through the probation officer, dealing with details of the case, motivations, intent and mitigating circumstances.

In endeavoring to respond to these questions, I am whipsawed in a variety of legalities. First, I may be called before a Senate Committee investigating this matter. Secondly, I may be involved in a civil suit, and thirdly there may be a new trial at some future date. Fourthly, the probation officer may be called before the Senate Committee to present testimony regarding what may otherwise be a privileged communication between defendant and Judge, as I understand it; if I answered certain questions to the probation officer, it is possible such answers could become a matter of record in the Senate and therefore available for use in the other proceedings just described. My answers would, it would seem to me, to violate my fifth amendment rights, and possibly my 6th amendment right to counsel and possibly other rights.

On the other hand, to fail to answer your questions may appear to be non-coopera- tion, and I can therefore expect a much more severe sentence.

There are further considerations which are not to be lightly taken. Several members of my family have expressed fear for my life if I disclose knowledge of the facts in this matter, either publicly or to any government representative. Whereas I do not share their concerns to the same degree, nevertheless, I do believe that retaliatory measures will be taken against me, my family, and my friends should I disclose such facts. Such retaliation could destroy careers, income, and reputations of persons who are innocent of any guilt whatever.

Be that as it may, in the interests of justice, and in the interests of restoring faith in the criminal justice system, which faith has been severely damaged in this case, I will state the following to you at this time which I hope may be of help to you in meting out justice in this case:

1. There was political pressure applied to the defendants to plead guilty and remain silent.

2. Perjury occurred during the trial in matters highly material to the very structure, orientation, and impact of the government's case, and to the motivation and intent of the defendants.

3. Others involved in the Watergate operation were not identified during the trial, when they could have been by those testifying.

James W. McCord wrote this March 1973 letter to Judge John Sirica, claiming that his testimony was given under pressure to "remain silent." It was this letter that implicated top Nixon administrators and intensified the Watergate scandal.

of his letter to Judge Sirica, which was interpreted as coopera- tion in the Watergate investigation, McCord's sentence was fur- ther suspended until June. (He was ultimately given a 5-year sentence, of which he served 3 months and 21 days.[91])

Because of the revelations in McCord's letter and mounting public suspicion about a possible cover-up, the Federal Grand Jury—with Sirica as presiding judge—reconvened on March 26 to reopen its Watergate investigation. The question at that point seemed not whether the Watergate cover-up would dissolve, but rather how quickly it would dissolve. The Plumbers were protecting the identities of more important, more powerful people than themselves, and the Grand Jury wanted those names. On March 30, Judge Sirica announced that the "Watergate Seven" (as the Plumbers were now known) would be granted immunity from further prosecution if they cooperated in the Watergate investigation. Behind closed doors, McCord was naming names. In a meeting with Sirica and Sam Dash—who was to be chief counsel in the impending Senate investigation of Watergate—McCord wrote a memo that Jeb Magruder had committed perjury during the federal trial and that, more important, he had been "involved in the Watergate operation sequence."[92] A bigger bombshell would follow a few days later: McCord revealed to *Los Angeles Times* reporter Robert Jackson that John Dean had been involved in the break-in and cover-up.[93] Magruder was merely an official of the Committee to Reelect the President, but John Dean was a big name—he was counsel to the president of the United States. On March 28, McCord would add a bigger name: In a closed door meeting with Sirica and Dash, McCord added the name of John Mitchell to the list of conspirators. Not only was Mitchell one of Nixon's closest friends, but also he was the former attorney general. The distance between the Plumbers and the White House was shrinking every day.

THE DOMINO EFFECT

For the next five weeks, the inner circle of advisers to the president—Haldeman, Ehrlichman, and Dean—all worked feverishly to contain the breach in the cover-up. How far would the Grand Jury go in its investigation of Watergate? Often meeting with one another in secret, sometimes calling one another and taping their phone conversations, other times meeting in conferences with the president, the conspirators frantically tried to construct a story that would (1) limit the fallout in the investigation, and (2) protect President Nixon. The primary strategy was to set up another "fall guy" for the Watergate break-in: What had materialized in the Watergate trial was the suggestion that Liddy was the boss of the operation, but McCord's revelations to Judge Sirica had destroyed that plan. After the trial, the president's men thought they might be able to set up Mitchell as the scapegoat. The Grand Jury investigation, and the media's tracking down of the facts in the case, however, destroyed the White House plans to protect itself. In April 1973, the awful truth began to emerge, and several top officials in the U.S. government resigned their posts.

The first to resign was Jeb Magruder. To reward his work for the CRP, President Nixon had given him a job as director of policy planning at the U.S. Department of Commerce. On April 26, after several weeks of testimony to the Grand Jury, testimony that revealed his involvement in the break-in and cover-up, Magruder resigned. He was the first domino to fall, and many more would follow. The following day, Pat Gray—humiliated in his Senate confirmation hearings—resigned as director of the FBI. On April 30, 1973, Richard Kleindienst announced his resignation as attorney general. Later that same day, the White House announced the resignation of the president's closest advisers: John Ehrlichman, H.R. Haldeman, and John Dean. The troubles for the White House, however, would only grow worse.

THE ERVIN COMMITTEE

The Senate Watergate Inquiry—which became known as the Ervin Committee (named for its chairman, Senator Sam Ervin)—began its proceedings on May 17, 1973. The Ervin Committee was different from the Grand Jury investigation. Although the Grand Jury was primarily interested in determining whether criminal activity had occurred in the Watergate case, the Ervin Committee was functioning as a "check" between the legislative and executive branches of the U.S. government. Though both the Grand Jury and the Ervin Committee were interested in getting to the truth of Watergate, the Ervin Committee was also trying to determine whether the executive branch (the president) had overstepped its boundaries. An anxious America watched as the proceedings were broadcast live on national television. In his opening statements, Senator Ervin set the tone for the proceedings, saying that the "aim of the committee is to provide full and open public testimony in order that the nation can proceed toward the healing of the wounds that now afflict the body politic."[94] The Ervin Committee's strategy was "to begin with the foot soldiers—the secretaries, the CREEP functionaries, the former New York cops—and move relentlessly upward in the ranks through the subalterns to the mighty commanders of Nixon's forces."[95]

Though the Ervin Committee's primary function was to investigate the Watergate break-in and cover-up, it was not a trial and held no legal authority. Congress is the legislative branch of government, not a court of law. Because the committee suspected that their investigation might reveal criminal activity, though, they set up an office, approved by the president himself, which would have the authority to prosecute any crimes uncovered during the investigation. As a result, any criminal activity revealed to the Ervin Committee would be forwarded to a judge called a "special prosecutor."

The special prosecutor would work closely with both the Senate hearings committee and the attorney general. Since the position was not permanent, the Senate had to find a legal expert to serve as special prosecutor. This section was very important: The prosecutor assigned to the hearings had to be impartial, fair, and highly qualified since it seemed likely that officials in the White House might be implicated in both the break-in and cover-up.

The man selected to the position was Archibald Cox, a famous law professor from Harvard University. Cox served as U.S. solicitor general (an attorney who advises the government, usually in Supreme Court cases) during the early 1960s; he was one of the most respected legal experts in the country. For the Ervin Committee, Cox was granted the power to investigate and prosecute any crimes revealed during the Inquiry: "The Special Prosecutor and a staff of his choosing would assume jurisdiction over a wide range of possible crimes: not only the Watergate bugging and cover-up, but 'all allegations involving the President, members of the White House staff, or Presidential appointees.'"[96] In addition, the special prosecutor would work without interference from the Executive Branch. Once Nixon had approved the appointment of Cox, he promised that neither he nor his new attorney general, Elliott Richardson (Richard Kleindienst had recently resigned in the wake of the Plumbers' trial), would meddle in the actions of the special prosecutor. Standing before the Ervin Committee, Richardson said,

> The Attorney General will not countermand or interfere with the Special Prosecutor's decisions or actions. The Special Prosecutor will determine whether and to what extent he will inform or consult with the Attorney General about the conduct of his duties and responsibilities. . . . The Special Prosecutor will not be removed from his duties except for extraordinary improprieties on his part.[97]

The special prosecutor's job, as was true for the entire Ervin Committee, was larger and far more important than merely the investigation of alleged crimes in the Watergate affair. Professor Cox and his staff were to perform their duties in an honest, straightforward manner in order to get to the truth. Cox understood the tremendous responsibility that he had in the Watergate investigation. In an interview with the *Washington Post*, he said, "This is a take of tremendous importance. Somehow we must restore confidence, honor, and integrity in government."[98]

A RECORDED REVELATION

The first two weeks of the Senate hearings revealed disturbing information about the White House involvement in Watergate, but a dramatic revelation about the cover-up occurred on June 1, 1973. That day, the committee's star witness, John Dean, who had grown weary of the cover-up operation and wanted to come clean about his involvement in the affair, revealed that he had had at least 35 different conversations about the break-in and cover-up with President Nixon himself. This information conflicted with President Nixon's frequent assertions that he had never even heard of the break-in before the trial of the Plumbers. Moreover, Dean said that Nixon's top advisers, John Ehrlichman and H.R. Haldeman, had been present during many of those meetings. Ehrlichman and Haldeman would soon be subpoenaed before the committee to verify Dean's accusations.

As dramatic as that development was, however, it was dwarfed by the information revealed on July 13, 1973. On that day, one of President Nixon's former aides, Alexander Butterfield, was called to testify. When a senator asked him if he knew whether Nixon had ever recorded any conversations in the White House, Butterfield said, "I was afraid you'd ask that question."[99] Butterfield then revealed to the Ervin Committee that, since 1971, Nixon had recorded all conversations and telephone calls in the White House! What was significant about Butterfield's revelation was that, if his testimony were correct, the 35 conversations that Dean was alleged to have had with the president would have been recorded.

Butterfield revealed to the committee that President Nixon began recording Oval Office conversations and phone calls as early as 1971 in order "to record things for posterity, for the Nixon library."[100] If Butterfield's revelation were true, then it

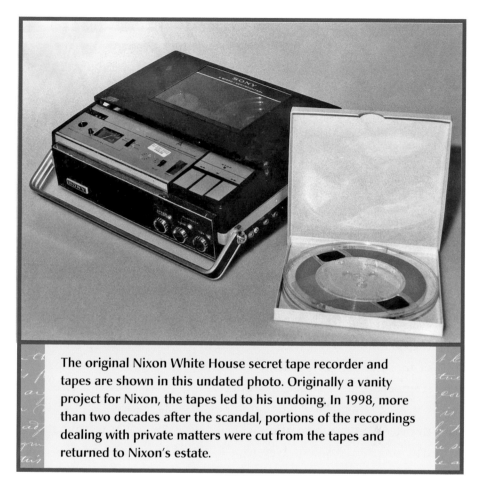

The original Nixon White House secret tape recorder and tapes are shown in this undated photo. Originally a vanity project for Nixon, the tapes led to his undoing. In 1998, more than two decades after the scandal, portions of the recordings dealing with private matters were cut from the tapes and returned to Nixon's estate.

would prove one of two possible outcomes: It would either exonerate the president, who had claimed on many occasions that he knew nothing about a cover-up, or it would implicate him and prove Dean's allegations that Nixon was a key decision maker in both the break-in and cover-up operations.

The Ervin Committee immediately demanded the tapes. What would happen as a result of the committee's demand opened a legal firestorm that would pit Congress against the White House and would ultimately bring the judicial branch of the U.S. government, the Supreme Court, into the fray. It was perhaps the greatest showdown among the three branches of government in the nation's history. Never before had all three branches of government been simultaneously involved in a power struggle. In the checks and balances system of U.S. government, usually only two branches would face off. But Watergate would pit the executive branch (the presidency) against the legislative *and* judicial branches (Congress and the Supreme Court).

5

The Supreme Court Intervenes

When the special prosecutor on the Ervin Committee, Archibald Cox, learned that President Nixon's conversations and telephone calls were recorded, he immediately instructed the Grand Jury (with Judge Sirica in charge) to issue a subpoena for the tapes. (A subpoena is a document that demands that a person or piece of evidence appear before a court.) On July 23, 1973, however, as the nation watched nervously, President Nixon refused to release them. As he had done during the Patrick Gray confirmation hearings, Nixon cited "executive privilege" for not releasing the tapes. A consultant to the president, Charles Alan Wright, wrote a letter to Cox explaining the president's refusal: "I am instructed by the President to inform you that it will not be possible to make available to you the recordings that you have requested."[101]

Cox was angry at Nixon's refusal to release the tapes. According to Cox, the president's refusal violated two elements of law. The first violation was that Cox himself considered the office of special prosecutor, though created at the request of the Ervin Committee, to be *part* of the Executive Branch. According to Nixon, the office of president granted him immunity (i.e., "executive privilege") from investigations conducted by either Congress or the Grand Jury. According to Cox, "executive privilege" did not apply in this case because the special prosecutor's office was technically affiliated with the executive—rather than judicial—branch of government. Wright countered this claim by saying that if Cox were a part of the executive branch, he would be "subject to the instructions of [his] superiors, up to and including the President, and can have access to [the tapes] only as and if the President sees fit to make them available to [him]."[102]

A second issue needed to be considered with regard to the notion of "executive privilege." Did the president, in fact, *have* the privilege to exempt himself from the Senate and Grand Jury subpoenas? That claim had gone unchallenged during the Patrick Gray FBI confirmation hearings, but, in the Watergate investigation, the stakes were much higher. During the hearings, Senator Ervin himself had remarked that "the Watergate tragedy is the greatest tragedy this country has ever suffered."[103] It was a sentiment that many Americans shared. What seemed at stake was trust in the government: The American people were worried that their leader, Richard Nixon, had not only authorized a spying operation on his political enemies but also had possibly tried to cover up any involvement that he and his advisers had in the affair. After reading Wright's letter, Cox angrily said, "Careful study before requesting the tapes convinced me that any blanket claim of privilege to withhold this evidence from a grand jury is without legal foundation."[104]

Nixon's refusal to release the tapes caused a nationwide uproar. According to Judge Sirica, "[T]he atmosphere in the country was growing more and more hostile toward the president."[105] Many people believed that Nixon was innocent, and, if so, any taped conversations would prove his innocence: "If the tapes were exculpatory of Nixon [i.e., proved his innocence], [he] would have made their existence known long before."[106] Nevertheless, despite public demand to release the tapes, the president stubbornly refused, asserting that the information on the tapes was a matter of national security and should under no circumstances be made public. Congress and the president—the legislative branch and the executive branch—were now at an impasse. It resembled a scene from a Western movie: Two gunfighters staring each other down. Who would win this showdown? The shootout, figurative rather than literal, would occur in courts of law.

AN EXECUTIVE COMPROMISE

Like the American public, both the Ervin Committee and the Grand Jury expressed outrage at the president's refusal to submit the tapes. In a letter demanding that the president reconsider his decision, Cox wrote, "The evidence on the tapes [. . .] may be material to public accusations against the respondent himself—a question to which he can hardly be indifferent [. . . .] From the earliest days of the Republic the courts have issued orders requiring executive officials to comply with the Constitution and laws as judicially interpreted."[107] In Cox's opinion, it was in the best interests of the nation for the tapes to be made public, and any claim of executive privilege was secondary

Archibald Cox stands on the Harvard University campus, where he taught at the school of law. A casualty of the notorious Watergate "Saturday Night Massacre," Cox famously said, "Whether ours shall be a government of laws and not of men is now for Congress and ultimately the American people to decide."

to the welfare of the American people. Judge Sirica agreed: "I was becoming increasingly suspicious that Nixon was more interested in protecting himself than in advancing the constitutional principles."[108]

After President Nixon's repeated refusals to release the tapes, the Grand Jury and Ervin Committee took the next step: a lawsuit. Although the president asserted that he was "answerable to the Nation but not the courts,"[109] on August 9, 1973, the Ervin Committee filed suit in the Washington, D.C., Federal Court demanding that Nixon relinquish the tapes. Having had his own subpoena refused by Nixon, Judge Sirica filed an appeal with the U.S. Court of Appeals on August 29. The Court of Appeals would announce its decision in six weeks.

AARON BURR

The Ervin Committee's subpoena to President Nixon was only the second time in American history that an acting president had been subpoenaed. The other incident had occurred in 1807, during the presidency of Thomas Jefferson. Aaron Burr (1756-1836), a famous American statesman, had served as vice president to Thomas Jefferson from 1801-1805, but not for Jefferson's second term. After leaving the vice presidency, Burr moved to what is now Louisiana and was alleged to have formed a conspiracy to overthrow the U.S. government. Certain letters were intercepted between Burr and ministers from Britain and Spain that suggested that Burr was planning to either overthrow the government or start a new country in the Western territories. In 1807, after Burr's letters were made public, he was charged with treason. In the subsequent trial, subpoenas were issued to President Jefferson to provide letters that were considered evidence in the case. Burr was ultimately acquitted because no witnesses came forward to testify against him.

The seven judges sitting on the Court of Appeals had to read hundreds of pages of documents from both sides of the issue. From the perspective of the Ervin Committee and Grand Jury, the desire to get to the truth of the Watergate affair outweighed any presidential claims to executive privilege. From the perspective of the White House, the executive branch was outside any court's jurisdiction. Despite that claim, on October 12, the Court of Appeals, upheld the Ervin Committee and Grand Jury's demand for the tapes. Public pressure on the White House was mounting.

As a result of the Court of Appeals' decision, President Nixon devised a compromise. Instead of releasing the tapes, he proposed to release transcriptions of the tapes. These transcriptions were to be heavily edited and then verified for accuracy by a Democratic senator, John C. Stennis. This plan was known as The Stennis Compromise. Initially, the Ervin Committee and Judge Sirica agreed to the compromise; however, Archibald Cox refused. Cox seemed to be continuously at odds with the White House—he was becoming a thorn in Nixon's side. Despite earlier promises not to interfere with the special prosecutor, Nixon began looking for ways to remove Cox from the position. Cox's refusal would set the stage for one of the most extraordinary events in American political history: The Saturday Night Massacre.

On Saturday, October 20, 1973, at a nationally televised press conference, Cox steadfastly refused to accept the Stennis Compromise. He said,

> I think it is my duty as special prosecutor, as an officer of the court, and as representative of the grand jury, to bring to the court's attention what seems to be noncompliance with the court's order [. . . .] Whether ours shall continue to be a government of laws and not of men is now for Congress and ultimately the American people to decide.[110]

Watching the televised press conference, Nixon became enraged. In his mind, the Stennis Compromise was an executive order, and Cox's refusal to accept it seemed like insubordination. Nixon immediately ordered his new attorney general, Elliott Richardson, to fire Cox. Richardson refused, telling the president, "I am acting on the basis of national interest as I see it."[111] Instead of carrying out the president's order, Richardson instead resigned his own position.

Now even more angry, Nixon called in the deputy attorney general, William Ruckelshaus, and ordered *him* to fire Cox. Like Richardson, Ruckelshaus refused; also, like Richardson, Ruckelshaus resigned rather than fire a man who appeared to be acting in the best interests of the country. The United States attorney general and deputy attorney general had all resigned their positions—would Nixon be able to find someone to fire Cox? Next in line was Solicitor General Robert Bork, who reluctantly agreed to dismiss Cox. Bork dutifully notified Cox that President Nixon had fired him. In one evening, three of the top officials in the U.S. government had lost their jobs. A stunned nation watched as the president's press secretary, Ron Ziegler, announced in a press conference the firing of Cox and the resignations of Richardson and Ruckelshaus. Moreover, Ziegler announced that the office of special prosecutor "has been abolished. Its function to investigate and prosecute those involved in the Watergate matter will be transferred back into the institutional framework of the Department of Justice."[112]

NIXON ON AMERICA'S BAD SIDE

The American people were furious at the president. Immediately, thousands of phone calls, telegrams, and letters began flooding the White House. According to Sam Dash, "Although the Watergate investigation had been noted for its bombshells, none had created such far-reaching, angry public shock waves as the firing of Special Prosecutor Cox and the resignations of

Richardson and Ruckelshaus. The country erupted in a wave of protest."[113] The president was quickly losing the support of the people who had, just a few months earlier, elected him to the White House. The Saturday Night Massacre was a devastating blow to Nixon's presidency.

Responding to national outrage, Nixon decided against abolishing the office of special prosecutor. About a week later, Leon Jaworski, a private attorney based in Texas, was named to the post. Interestingly, although Cox himself had been fired, his staff at the special prosecutor's office had remained intact. They were very suspicious of the new special prosecutor, though: Would he be interested in justice, or would he be another guy like Pat Gray, that is, someone who would do the president's bidding, no matter what? Cox's assistant, Richard Ben-Veniste, said, "To say that we had very little confidence in our new boss, Leon Jaworski, on the day he was sworn in would be putting it mildly."[114] As it turned out, however, Jaworski was just as dogged in his investigation as Cox had been. If Nixon had been hoping for an easily manipulated special prosecutor, he was wrong in his choice of Jaworski.

To calm the nation's anxieties about the tapes, President Nixon agreed to release three of the subpoenaed tapes to Judge Sirica on November 26, 1973. The tapes were heavily edited; many portions had been erased. Three weeks later, a frustrated Sirica ruled that he would not turn over the tapes to the special prosecutor because none of the information on them pertained to Watergate. Sirica then demanded a more complete subpoena of Nixon recordings: The Grand Jury now asked for 500 White House tapes.

The year 1973 had started well for President Nixon—he had won the presidency with an overwhelming majority vote, and his inauguration in January had been a glorious celebration. The future had looked bright for Nixon, but by the end of the year, things were looking grim. As a result of the Grand

Jury and Ervin Committee investigations, and Nixon's stubborn assertions of executive privilege, many Congressmen were calling for Nixon's resignation. Democrats as well as Republicans began calling for an impeachment. Watergate had cast a shadow on the presidency. Unfortunately for Nixon, 1974 would be even worse.

On February 6, 1974, after two months of the president's continuous refusal to release more tapes to authorities, the U.S. House of Representatives voted to approve an investigation into whether the House had enough evidence to impeach Nixon. It was now no longer merely a national curiosity: Watergate had exploded into a national crisis.

On February 19, 1974, the Ervin Committee officially ended its public hearings. The Senate committee would now yield

IMPEACHMENTS

An impeachment is a process by which the House of Representatives may accuse a government official of misconduct. As specified in the U.S. Constitution (Article 1, sections 2 and 3), the House of Representatives can accuse an incumbent president of criminal activity. If an article of impeachment "passes" the House—that is, if a majority of Representatives approve the impeachment—the accusation moves to the Senate, which has the Constitutional authority to remove the president "for, and conviction of, treason, bribery, or other high crimes and misdemeanors" (Article 2, Section 4). In more than 200 years of United States history, only two Presidents have been impeached: Andrew Johnson in 1868 and Bill Clinton in 1998. It should be noted that an impeachment is not a conviction; rather, it is a formal accusation of criminal activity. Once a government official is impeached by the House of Representatives, the Senate then has the authority to convict him.

to the authority of the courts and to the House of Representatives Judiciary Committee. The Ervin Committee believed
it had compiled enough evidence to get to the bottom of the
Watergate conspiracy: It believed it had rooted out all the perpetrators in the break-in and cover-up. The special prosecutor's
office was still working diligently alongside the Grand Jury to
procure the presidential tapes and also to indict the remaining
conspirators. Those conspirators were Charles Colson, Robert
Mardian, Kenneth Parkinson, Gordon Strachan, John Ehrlichman, H.R. Haldeman, and John Mitchell. One obvious name
was missing from the list, however—Richard M. Nixon. Rather
than name him as a conspirator, the special prosecutor's office
referred to him as "an unindicted coconspirator"—a term that
would become famous. In other words, the special prosecutor's
office believed that Nixon was involved in the conspiracy but
perhaps not enough to warrant an indictment. On March 1,
1974, the Grand Jury formally handed down indictments to the
seven former White House aides. They were charged with "attempting to cover up the Watergate investigation by lying to the
FBI and the Grand Jury and with payments of hush money to
the original defendants."[115] According to Richard Ben-Veniste,
"Never had so many powerful and close associates of an American President been charged with crime."[116] Regardless of what
would happen during the court proceedings of the Watergate
conspirators, however, the person *really* on trial was the president of the United States.

Meanwhile, the president continued to stonewall requests
for the tapes. The Ervin Committee and Grand Jury had both
successfully appealed to the U.S. Court of Appeals to force
Nixon to release the tapes, but no tapes were forthcoming.
Nixon continued to assert executive privilege. The Watergate
crisis was moving into a new phase, though: It was now out
of the hands of the Grand Jury, and now into the halls of the
U.S. Congress. On April 11, 1974, the House of Representatives Judiciary Committee—convened to determine whether

there was enough evidence to impeach Nixon—demanded 42 tapes from the White House. It was a strong-arm tactic: If Nixon refused, he could then be impeached on the grounds of "Contempt of Congress."

THE PRESIDENT'S FINAL MOVE

Nixon was desperate—his final ploy was to try to release summaries of the subpoenaed tapes, rather than word-for-word transcripts or the tapes themselves. The special prosecutor's office and Judge Sirica both agreed to Nixon's compromise, and, on April 29, 1974, Nixon's staff released edited summaries of 46 taped conversations. Nixon boasted that the summaries would "at last, once and for all, show that what I knew and did in regard to the Watergate break-in and cover-up were just as I have described them to you from the beginning."[117] The summaries were immediately released to the public, and in fact became best-selling books.

Nixon's strategy backfired, however: He had hoped that the summaries would exonerate him, but they instead had the opposite effect. They made him seem even more guilty than before the summaries were released. The summaries were clearly insufficient and obviously slanted toward making the president seem innocent. A Republican senator, Hugh Scott, called them "shabby, disgusting, immoral."[118] As harsh as the public reaction was to the Nixon plan, the House Judiciary Committee was even harsher: They clearly did not believe, as the president had hoped they would, that the summaries offered were in compliance with the subpoenas. A few days after Nixon submitted the summaries, the Chairman of the Judiciary Committee, Representative Peter Rodino, wrote a letter to the president: "Dear Mr. President: The committee on the Judiciary has directed me to advise you that it finds as of 10:00 A.M. April 30, you have failed to comply with the Committee's subpoena of April 11, 1974."[119]

The Judiciary Committee, obviously, was not satisfied with Nixon's summaries. After sending the letter to the president,

IN THE UNITED STATES DISTRICT COURT
FOR THE DISTRICT OF COLUMBIA

SENATE SELECT COMMITTEE ON PRESIDENTIAL
CAMPAIGN ACTIVITIES, suing in its own
name and in the name of the UNITED
STATES,

and

SAM J. ERVIN, JR.; HOWARD H. BAKER, JR.;
HERMAN E. TALMADGE; DANIEL K. INOUYE;
JOSEPH M. MONTOYA; EDWARD J. GURNEY;
and LOWELL P. WEICKER, JR., as United
States Senators who are members of the
Senate Select Committee on Presidential
Campaign Activities.

United States Senate
Washington, D.C. 20510

Plaintiffs

v.

RICHARD M. NIXON, individually and as
President of the United States.

The White House
Washington, D.C. 20500

Defendant

Civil
Action
No.

COMPLAINT FOR DECLARATORY JUDGMENT,
MANDATORY INJUNCTION AND MANDAMUS

Respectfully submitted,

Samuel Dash
Chief Counsel

Fred D. Thompson
Minority Counsel

Rufus L. Edmisten
Deputy Counsel

James Hamilton
Assistant Chief Counsel

William T. Mayton
Assistant Counsel

Ronald D. Rotunda
Assistant Counsel

Sherman Cohn
Eugene Gressman
Jerome A. Barron
   Washington, D. C.
Of Counsel

Arthur S. Miller
   Chief Consultant to
   the Select Committee
   Washington, D. C.
Of Counsel

United States Senate
Washington, D. C.   20510
Telephone Number 225-0531

The first and last pages of the complaint (*left*) filed in federal court in Washington, D.C., by the Senate Watergate Committee are shown at left. The complaint names as defendant Richard M. Nixon, individually and as president of the United States.

they immediately subpoenaed the 42 tapes themselves, so that the conversations on them could be compared with the summaries offered by Nixon's staff. Nixon's gamble had failed. After the edited summaries were released, the Judiciary Committee issued two additional subpoenas for the tapes, the final one on May 30, 1974. As he had before, Nixon refused.

Meanwhile, the federal trial of *United States v. John N. Mitchell, et al.* (the trial of the seven Watergate conspirators identified by the Grand Jury)[120] was issuing its own subpoena for the Watergate tapes. On May 20, 1974, Judge Sirica—presiding in the new trial as he had done in the Plumbers' trial—issued his final subpoena. In response, Nixon's attorneys immediately drafted an appeal to the U.S. Court of Appeals in an attempt to block access to the tapes. It had been a predictable, frustrating routine since the previous July.

At that point, Special Prosecutor Jaworski had run out of patience. The Ervin Committee, the Grand Jury, the Federal Court, the Appeals Courts, and the U.S. Congress had all failed to force Nixon to release the Watergate tapes. Jaworski then played his final card: He appealed to the U.S. Supreme Court to rule on the issue. In an unusual move, he asked the Supreme Court to rule *before* the Court of Appeals had announced its decision on Nixon's appeal. The normal procedure for the Supreme Court's agreeing to hear a case is for the appeals process to be "exhausted," meaning that all other appeals had to have been made (in legal terms, "adjudicated") before the case could go to the Supreme Court. Jaworski believed, however, that the Watergate crisis warranted a speedy intervention. The Supreme Court agreed, believing that Watergate constituted a "checks and balances" crisis among the three branches of government.

Jaworski filed a writ of certiorari (a petition for a court to hear a case) to the U.S. Supreme Court on June 7, 1974. The purpose of the "writ" was to bring in the Supreme Court to rule on the issue of "executive privilege." Although President Nixon had continuously cited executive privilege to deny access to the Watergate tapes, Jaworski was unconvinced that Nixon indeed had that power, at least to the degree that he was claiming he did.

EXECUTIVE PRIVILEGE VERSUS CHECKS AND BALANCES

Normally, it takes months for the Supreme Court to grant certiorari, that is, approve the "writ," in a particular case (and, it should be noted, far fewer than 10 percent of writs of certiorari to the Supreme Court are ever granted), but in *United States v. Nixon*, the Supreme Court agreed to expedite the case. That is, the Court agreed to proceed more quickly than usual. Perhaps a primary reason the Supreme Court agreed to hear the case was that the U.S. House of Representatives was initiating its impeachment procedure against the president. A secondary reason was that the federal trial of *United States v. John N. Mitchell, et al.*, had stalled because the still-unreleased tapes would provide the crucial evidence in that case. The most important reason that the Supreme Court granted certiorari in this case, however, was that it believed *United States v. Nixon* dealt with a critical issue of constitutional law: Who gets to decide what is constitutional—the president or the Supreme Court? A speedy decision on the issue of executive privilege seemed appropriate.

The Supreme Court is the highest legal authority in the United States. Nine judges, called "justices," sit on the Supreme Court. They are specially nominated by the president. Once nominated, they must be approved by the U.S. Congress. Once approved by Congress, they cannot be removed from their positions: They can sit on the Supreme Court for as long as they live. They are the final legal authority in the country. The nine justices on the Supreme Court in 1974 were William O. Douglas, William J. Brennan, William Rehnquist, Potter Stewart, Byron R. White, Thurgood Marshall, Harry A. Blackmun, Lewis F. Powell, and Chief Justice Warren Burger. There was a strange twist to the case: Because Supreme Court justices are nominated by the president, there were three judges on the court nominated by Nixon himself—Chief Justice

Burger, Justice Rehnquist, and Justice Blackmun. Would those justices be loyal to the President? Or would they set aside their gratitude to Nixon and deal dispassionately with the evidence in the case? One of the justices, Rehnquist, was such a close friend of Nixon's that he recused himself from the trial, declining to participate in the proceedings.

The special prosecutor's writ of certiorari posed five questions to the Supreme Court:

1. Whether the president, when he has assumed sole personal and physical control over evidence demonstrably material to the trial of charges of obstruction of justice in a federal court, is subject to a judicial order directing compliance with a subpoena [. . .] issued on the application of the special prosecutor in the name of the United States.

2. Whether a federal court is bound by the assertion by the president of an absolute "executive privilege" to withhold demonstrably material evidence from the trial of charges of obstruction of justice by his own White House aides and party leaders, upon the ground that he deems production to be against the public interest.

3. Whether a claim of executive privilege based on the generalized interest in the confidentiality of government deliberations can block the prosecution's access to evidence.

4. Whether any executive privilege that otherwise might have been applicable to discussions in the offices of the president concerning the Watergate matter has been waived by previous testimony pursuant to the president's public release of 1,216 pages of edited transcript of forty-three Presidential conversations relating to Watergate.

5. Whether the district court properly determined that a subpoena [. . .] issued to the president satisfies the standards of Rule 17(c) of the Federal Rules of Criminal Procedure because an adequate showing has been made that the subpoenaed items are relevant to issues to be tried and will be admissable in evidence.[121]

The key questions, of course, were numbers 2–4, which pertained to "executive privilege."

Although it often takes several months between the time the Supreme Court grants certiorari and the time the Supreme Court hears the case, *United States v. Nixon* was moved up because it represented such an important issue regarding constitutional law. Case number 73-1766, *United States of America, Petitioner v. Richard M. Nixon, President of the United States, Petitioner, et al.,* began on Monday, July 8, 1974, barely one month after Jaworski had filed his writ of certiorari.

In his opening arguments to the Supreme Court, Jaworski quickly got to the key issue of the case. "[W]hen boiled down," he said to the justices seated in the Supreme Court Building, "this case really presents one fundamental issue. Who is to be the arbiter of what the Constitution says?"[122] In the "checks and balances" system, the Supreme Court has the final word on whether an issue is constitutional. Jaworski believed that President Nixon (the executive branch)—instead of the Supreme Court—was trying to determine the constitutionality of executive privilege. It was, indeed, the crucial question. For more than a year, Nixon had been citing executive privilege as a constitutionally authorized right to withhold the Watergate tapes, but did he in fact have that privilege? Moreover, did the executive branch have the right to determine whether executive privilege was indeed constitutional? Jaworski continued, "Now, the President may be right in how he reads the Constitution. But he may also be wrong. And if he is wrong, who is there to tell him so?"[123]

The July 22, 1974, cover of *Time* magazine shows the importance the Watergate scandal took on. Nixon's refusal to turn over his tape recordings called into question the limits of executive privilege, a matter the U.S. Supreme Court would decide.

The next issue concerned whether the president even has executive privilege. Barely five minutes into Jaworski's opening arguments, Justice William O. Douglas asked him, "Well, we start with a Constitution that does not contain the words 'executive privilege,' is that right?" This was an interesting development in the case: Although Nixon had persistently asserted "executive privilege," the fact of the matter was that the Constitution did not grant such a privilege, at least not in those words. For several minutes, the justices and Jaworski tried to determine what "executive privileges" were available to the president. They all seemed to agree that the executive branch should have certain privileges, especially, as Jaworski said, "in some situations [. . .] where military secrets and such as that were involved, or

🔨 GRANTING CERTIORARI

It bears repeating that almost all writs of certiorari to the U.S. Supreme Court are turned down. In the early 1970s, for example, the Supreme Court received more than 2000 writs per year, of which fewer than 150 per year were granted. For any particular appeal to be argued before the Supreme Court, the justices of the Supreme Court had developed a procedure called the "Rule of Four": "For a case to be selected for review at least four members must agree that an appeal deserves to be granted full consideration of the entire court because it presents an important issue of federal or constitutional law."* In other words, if at least four of the nine Supreme Court justices agree to hear the case, they will grant certiorari and schedule the appeal.

---

* Paul B. Wice, *Miranda v. Arizona: "You Have the Right to Remain Silent . . ."* (New York: Franklin Watts, 1996) 30.

national secrets of great importance."[124] It was clear that Jaworski's oral arguments centered on the issue of executive privilege: How much, ultimately, does the president have?

Representing the president in the case was James D. St. Clair, Nixon's personal attorney. In his opening arguments to the justices, St. Clair asked that the case be immediately dismissed because Nixon's appeal to the U.S. District Court of Appeals had not yet been adjudicated. In other words, because all appeals had not yet been exhausted, the Supreme Court should have no interest in Nixon. The Supreme Court justices had little patience with this line of argument and steered St. Clair toward the central issue of the Watergate crisis: the president's refusal to release the tapes, and the fact that House of Representatives was initiating impeachment proceedings against the president:

> QUESTION: What in those tapes involves the impeachment proceedings?
> MR. ST. CLAIR: Pardon?
> QUESTION: What in any of these tapes is involved in the impeachment proceeding?
> MR. ST. CLAIR: Well, if Your Honor please, the House of Representatives has subpoenaed—
> QUESTION: I don't know what is in the tapes. I assume you do.
> MR. ST. CLAIR: No, I don't.
> QUESTION: You don't know, either. Well, how do you know that they are subject to executive privilege?[125]

There, in one short, tense exchange between the Supreme Court and the president's attorney appeared the central issue of the case: Was it the President's prerogative (right) to determine whether an item was subject to executive privilege, or, rather, was it the Supreme Court's prerogative?

THE PRESIDENT STEPS DOWN

The presentation of arguments to the Supreme Court lasted two days. After the arguments, the Supreme Court justices met behind closed doors to determine the outcome of the case. It is a solemn duty that has been enacted hundreds of times in the history of the United States. Very few of the Supreme Court's decisions, however—and there had been thousands handed down since the Supreme Court had been instituted on February 1, 1790—dealt so closely with the checks and balances element of American government. The case of *United States v. Nixon* served a larger role than just as a ruling on whether or not the president could withhold the Watergate tapes; what was at stake was protecting the checks and balances system of the U.S. government. If the president had the sole right to determine what constituted executive privilege, how far could that right extend? Was the president ultimately stronger than the other two branches of government?

After a case is argued before the Supreme Court, the justices vote on the outcome. That's why there are nine justices: to ensure that there will always be a majority vote. With one justice, Rehnquist, excusing himself from the proceedings, though, would there be a tie? Sometimes, the justices will deliberate for several weeks to come to a decision on a case. The justices on *United States v. Nixon* needed only two weeks to deliberate, however, and they came to a unanimous decision. By a vote of 8–0, they ruled against Nixon. As a result of the ruling, all claims of executive privilege to withhold the Watergate tapes were denied. Furthermore, and more important, "The court rejected the President's claims of absolute executive privilege."[126]

The clearest statement in the Supreme Court's written decision on the case was this: "The judiciary, not the President, was the final arbiter of a claim of executive privilege."[127] This statement was very important because it settled the three branches of government that had for two years appeared out of balance.

Under threat of impending impeachment, Richard M. Nixon resigned from the presidency, as reflected in this August 9, 1974, front page of the *New York Times*. Nixon's vice president, Gerald Ford, assumed the office, and Nixon retreated in shame.

President Nixon's persistent refusal to submit to the courts' subpoenas had seemed to an anxious nation that the executive branch of the U.S. government was declaring itself more important—more powerful—than the other two branches.

The Supreme Court's decision was devastating to President Nixon. There was now no way to avoid having to submit the Watergate tapes to the House of Representatives' Judiciary Committee. Impeachment was imminent. On August 6, 1974, President Nixon sat in the Oval Office and listened to several of the tapes over and over again. He realized that they were incriminating rather than exonerating. If the House of Representatives heard those tapes, they would surely have enough evidence to impeach him. Once impeached, he would be found guilty in the Senate of committing crimes against the United States. There was no way out. So on August 8, 1974, on national television, Richard M. Nixon resigned as president of the United States. He is the only president ever to have resigned while still in office. What had seemed in the summer of 1972 as merely a bungled robbery attempt ultimately became one of the most significant events in the history of the United States.

Chronology

November 5, 1968	Richard Nixon is elected thirty-seventh president of the United States.
June 17, 1972	Five members of "the Plumbers," a seven-member espionage group working for the Committee to Reelect the President, are arrested for attempting to break into the Democratic National Committee headquarters in the Watergate Hotel.
August 1, 1972	It is reported in the *Washington Post* that a $25,000 check written to the Committee to Reelect the President wound up in the bank account of one of the five men arrested in the Watergate break-in.
November 7, 1972	Nixon is reelected.
January 30, 1973	G. Gordon Liddy, E. Howard Hunt, and the other five Plumbers are convicted of conspiracy, burglary, and wiretapping.
April 30, 1973	Nixon's highest-ranking aides, H.R. Haldeman and John Ehrlichman, in addition to the attorney general, Richard Kleindienst, resign over mounting suspicions of their involvement in the Watergate scandal.
May 18, 1973	The Senate Watergate Committee begins nationally televised hearings. Archibald Cox is named special prosecutor.
June 3, 1973	John Dean, former special counsel to the president, reveals to the Senate committee that he had 35 separate conversations about Watergate with President Nixon.

July 13, 1973	One of Nixon's aides, Alexander Butterfield, reveals to the Senate committee that all conversations and telephone calls in the White House since 1971 had been recorded.
July 23, 1973	Citing "executive privilege," Nixon refuses to turn the White House tapes over to the Senate.
October 20, 1973	In the "Saturday Night Massacre," Nixon fires Archibald Cox, and Attorney General Elliott Richardson and Assistant Attorney General William D. Ruckelshaus resign. About a week later, Leon Jaworski is named new special prosecutor.

Timeline

April 30, 1973
Nixon's highest ranking aides, H.R. Haldeman and John Ehrlichman, in addition to the attorney general, Richard Kleindienst, resign over mounting suspicions of their involvement in the Watergate scandal.

November 5, 1968
Richard Nixon is elected thirty-seventh president of the United States.

1968

1973

June 17, 1972
Five members of "the Plumbers," a seven-member espionage group working for the Committee to Reelect the President, are arrested for attempting to break into the Democratic National Committee headquarters in the Watergate Hotel.

May 18, 1973
The Senate Watergate Committee begins nationally televised hearings. Archibald Cox is named special prosecutor.

April 30, 1974   Nixon releases a 1,200-page, edited
                  manuscript of the White House tapes
                  to the House of Representatives Judiciary
                  Committee. The Committee, however,
                  demands that Nixon release the
                  tapes themselves.

June 7, 1974   New Special Prosecutor Leon Jaworski
                  files a writ of certiorari to the U.S.
                  Supreme Court to rule on the issue of
                  "executive privilege."

July 8, 1974   The Supreme Court case, *United States v.
                  Richard Nixon*, begins.

July 13, 1973
One of Nixon's aides, Alexander
Butterfield, reveals to the Senate
committee that all conversations
and telephone calls in the
White House since 1971 had
been recorded.

July 24, 1974
The Supreme Court rules
unanimously against the
president and demands
that Nixon release the
White House tapes.

1973

1974

July 8, 1974
The Supreme Court
case, *United States v.
Richard Nixon*, begins.

August 8, 1974
Nixon becomes
the first U.S.
president to resign
while in office.

July 24, 1974	The Supreme Court rules unanimously against the president and demands that Nixon release the White House tapes.
July 27, 1974	The House of Representatives Judiciary Committee passes the first of three articles of impeachment against President Nixon.
August 8, 1974	Nixon becomes the first U.S. president to resign while in office.

Notes

1. "Its tenants included the former Attorney General of the United States John N. Mitchell [and] the former Secretary of Commerce Maurice H. Stans." Carl Bernstein and Bob Woodward, *All the President's Men.* New York: Simon and Schuster, 1974, p. 14. Both Mitchell and Stans were key players in the subsequent scandal.

2. G. Gordon Liddy, *Will.* New York: St. Martin's, 1980, p. 245.

3. Bernstein and Woodward, *All the President's Men,* p. 16.

4. See Barry Sussman, *The Great Cover-Up: Nixon and The Scandal of Watergate.* New York: Thomas Y. Crowell, 1974, p. 5.

5. See J. Anthony Lukas, *Nightmare: The Underside of the Nixon Years.* New York: Viking, 1976, pp. 77–78. Among his pseudonyms were David St. John, John Baxter, Gordon Davis, and Robert Dietrich.

6. Quoted in Lukas, *Nightmare,* p. 79.

7. Ibid., p. 108.

8. Ibid., p. 208.

9. Ibid., p. 212.

10. Richard Ben-Veniste and George Frampton, Jr., *Stonewall: The Real Story of the Watergate Prosecution.* New York: Simon and Schuster, 1977, p. 11.

11. Quoted in Lukas, *Nightmare,* pp. 213–214. Liddy's account of the conversation differs slightly from Magruder's; see Liddy, *Will,* p. 250.

12. Quoted in Fred Emery, *Watergate: The Corruption of American Politics and the Fall of Richard Nixon.* New York: Times Books, 1994, p. 153.

13. Quoted in Jeb Stuart Magruder, *An American Life: One Man's Journey to Watergate.* New York: Atheneum, 1974, pp. 214–215.

14. Emery, *Watergate,* p. 10.

15. Lukas, *Nightmare,* p. 217.

16. Magruder, *An American Life,* p. 222.

17. Quoted in Emery, *Watergate,* p. 159.

18. Richard M. Nixon, *RN: The Memoirs of Richard Nixon.* New York: Grosset & Dunlap, 1975, p. 627.

19. Quoted in Emery, *Watergate,* p. 161.

20. See New York Times Staff, *The End of a Presidency.* New York: Bantam, 1974, p. 132.

21. Quoted in Magruder, *An American Life,* p. 225.

22. Lukas, *Nightmare,* p. 221.

23. In his book, *Justice,* Kleindienst claims that he was not at the June 20 meeting, but Ehrlichman, Haldeman, and Dean all assert that he was present.

24. Lukas, *Nightmare,* p. 225.

25. Gordon Strachan was the liaison officer between Haldeman and the Committee to Reelect the President. In the subsequent Watergate hearings, all charges against Strachan were dropped.

26. Quoted in Lukas, *Nightmare,* p. 227.

27. Lukas, *Nightmare,* p. 176.

28. Emery, *Watergate,* p. 182.

29. *Watergate* TV series, May 1993.

30. Ehrlichman denies this charge: See John Ehrlichman, *Witness to Power.* New York: Simon and Schuster, 1982, p. 342–343.

31. Quoted in John Dean, *Blind Ambition,* New York: Simon and Schuster, 1976, p. 221.

32. Emery, *Watergate,* pp. 182–183.

33. Liddy refers to him as the "damage control action officer" (Liddy, *Will,* p. 250).

34. Dean, *Blind Ambition,* p. 119.

35. J. Edgar Hoover, the previous FBI director, held the job from 1924 till his death on May 2, 1972. Gray was the "interim" director, meaning that he would hold the job temporarily until a successor to Hoover could be found.

36. Dean, *Blind Ambition,* p. 122.

37. Emery, *Watergate,* p. 186.

38. Lukas, *Nightmare,* p. 229.

39. Ibid., p. 229.

40. Quoted in Emery, *Watergate,* p. 190.

41. Emery, *Watergate,* p. 194.

42. Lukas, *Nightmare,* p. 236.

43. Magruder, *An American Life,* p. 224.

44. Dean, *Blind Ambition,* p. 131.

45. Lukas, *Nightmare,* p. 249.

46. Magruder, *An American Life,* p. 224.

47. Emery, *Watergate,* p. 195.

48. Lukas, *Nightmare,* p. 253.

49. Dean, *Blind Ambition,* p. 131.

50. Quoted in Lukas, *Nightmare*, p. 254.

51. Dean, *Blind Ambition*, p. 127.

52. Ibid., p. 133.

53. Ibid., p. 137.

54. John J. Sirica, *To Set the Record Straight: The Break-in, the Tapes, the Conspirators, the Pardon.* New York: Norton, 1979, p. 52.

55. Sirica, *To Set the Record Straight*, p. 37.

56. Ibid., p. 52.

57. Emery, *Watergate*, p. 224.

58. Quoted in Emery, *Watergate*, p. 257.

59. Ibid., p. 257.

60. Dean, *Blind Ambition*, p. 154.

61. Quoted in Dean, *Blind Ambition*, p. 157.

62. Dean, *Blind Ambition*, p. 162.

63. Lukas, *Nightmare*, p. 259.

64. Ibid., p. 259. See, also, Dean, *Blind Ambition*, pp. 164–165 and H.R. Haldeman and Joseph DiMona, *The Ends of Power.* New York: Times Books, 1978, p. 222.

65. Quoted in Lukas, *Nightmare*, pp. 261–262.

66. Sirica, *To Set the Record Straight*, p. 61.

67. Sirica, *To Set the Record Straight*, p. 67.

68. Ibid., p. 57.

69. Quoted in Sirica, *To Set the Record Straight*, p. 63.

70. Sirica, *To Set the Record Straight*, p. 69.

71. Ibid., p. 70.

72. Two articles appeared in national newspapers that week alleging that the Plumbers were being bullied into guilty pleas and being paid to remain silent. See Seymour Hersh, "Pressure to Plead Guilty Alleged in Watergate Case," *New York Times* (January 15, 1973): pp. 1–2; and Jack Anderson, "Watergate Defendants Might Talk," *Washington Post* (January 11, 1973): p. G17.

73. Quoted in Magruder, *An American Life*, p. 280.

74. Sirica, *To Set the Record Straight*, p. 74.

75. Ibid., p. 86.

76. Ibid., p. 88.

77. Quoted in Lukas, *Nightmare*, p. 278.

78. Quoted in Emery, *Watergate*, p. 287.

79. Emery, *Watergate*, p. 287.

80. Quoted in Lukas, *Nightmare*, p. 247.

81. See E. Howard Hunt, *Undercover: Memoirs of an American Secret Agent.* New York: Berkeley, 1974, pp. 294–296.

82. Ibid., p. 295.

83. Dean, *Blind Ambition,* pp. 192–193.

84. Hunt, *Undercover,* p. 297.

85. Quoted in Sirica, *To Set the Record Straight,* p. 96.

86. Sirica, *To Set the Record Straight,* p. 97.

87. Ibid., p. 108.

88. Emery, *Watergate,* p. 270.

89. Sirica, *To Set the Record Straight,* pp. 117–118.

90. A "provisional" sentence is different than a "final" sentence. A provisional sentence is given to a defendant with the understanding that a final sentence will come later, that is, after a "final study" of the case being tried. Judge Sirica explains it this way: "The statute [governing provisional sentencing] provided that maximum sentences be imposed for the period during which further study was going on. I never had any attention whatsoever of putting those men in jail for thirty to forty years" (Sirica, *To Set the Record Straight,* p. 118). Liddy's sentence on March 23, 1972, was a "final" sentence. In November, 1973, Sirica imposed final sentences on Hunt and the Miamians. Hunt was given an eight-year sentence; the Miamians were given four-year sentences. Hunt's prison sentence was reduced to 31 months. None of the Miamians served more than 14 months.

91. Sirica believes that without McCord's letter Watergate would have remained covered up: "In my opinion, this case would never have been broken if McCord had elected to stand pat and not written the letter to me." (Ibid., p. 116)

92. Quoted in Emery, *Watergate,* p. 273.

93. See Robert L. Jackson, "Hunt Partly Backs McCord Testimony," *Los Angeles Times* (April 4, 1973): p. A1+.

94. Quoted in New York Times Staff, *The End of a Presidency,* p. 209.

95. Lukas, *Nightmare,* p. 341.

96. Ben-Veniste and Frampton, *Stonewall,* p. 17.

97. Frank Mankiewicz, *U.S. v. Richard Nixon.* New York: Quadrangle, 1975, p. 15.

98. Quoted in George Lardner, "Cox Is Chosen as Special Prosecutor," *Washington Post* (May 19, 1973) p. A1.

99. Quoted in Frank Mankiewicz, *U.S. v. Richard Nixon,* p. 27.

100. Quoted in Lawrence Meyer, "President Taped Talks, Phone Calls," *Washington Post* (July 17, 1973): p. A1.

101. Quoted in Carroll Kilpatrick, "President Refuses to Turn Over Tapes; Ervin Committee, Cox Issue Subpoenas," *Washington Post* (July 24, 1973): p. A1.

102. Ibid., p. A1.

103. Ibid., p. A1.

104. Ibid., p. A1.

105. Sirica, *To Set the Record Straight*, p. 156.

106. Mankiewicz, *U.S. v. Richard Nixon*, p. 24.

107. Quoted in Sirica, *To Set the Record Straight*, p. 150.

108. Sirica, *To Set the Record Straight*, p. 153.

109. Quoted in New York Times Staff, *The End of a Presidency*, p. 222.

110. Quoted in Lukas, *Nightmare*, pp. 436, 440.

111. Ibid., p. 437.

112. Ibid., p. 440.

113. Sam Dash, *Chief Counsel: Inside the Ervin Committee—The Untold Story of Watergate*, New York: Random House, 1976, p. 212.

114. Ben-Veniste and Frampton, *Stonewall*, p. 187.

115. New York Times Staff, *The End of a Presidency*, p. 243.

116. Ben-Veniste and Frampton, *Stonewall*, p. 255.

117. Quoted in Emery, *Watergate*, p. 429.

118. Ibid., p. 430.

119. Quoted in Mankiewicz, *U.S. v. Richard Nixon*, p. 230.

120. The key Watergate conspirators were all found guilty of various criminal charges. Charles Colson served seven months in prison on obstruction of justice charges. John Dean served four months in prison on perjury charges. John Ehrlichman and H.R. Haldeman each served 18 months in jail on obstruction of justice and perjury charges. Jeb Magruder spent seven months in jail on conspiracy and perjury charges. Robert Mardian was convicted but successfully appealed based on legal technicalities related to his trial. Kenneth Parkinson was acquitted. In Gordon Strachan's trial, all charges against him were dropped. The big fish, John Mitchell, was found guilty of conspiracy, obstruction of justice, and perjury, and

sentenced to eight years in prison.

121. Quoted in Leo Friedman, ed., *United States v. Nixon: The President Before the Supreme Court.* New York: Chelsea House, 1974, p. 172.

122. *United States v. Nixon,* p. 528.

123. Ibid., p. 528.

124. Ibid., p. 540.

125. Ibid., pp. 549–550.

126. Ibid., p. 598.

127. Ibid., p. 600.

Glossary

appeals (appellate) court A court of law that considers appeals to legal decisions handed down from lower courts. Each state in the United States has at least one appellate court. The highest appellate court in the United States is the Supreme Court.

checks and balances A system set up in U.S. government that attempts to guarantee equality among the three branches of government (executive, legislative, and judicial). All three branches of government have certain powers that can limit (or "check") the powers of the other branches.

Committee to Reelect the President An agency, separate from the Republican Party, whose task was to ensure the reelection of Richard Nixon in 1972. Also called CRP or CREEP.

defendant The party accused in a court of law.

executive privilege The alleged right of the president of the United States to exempt himself from criminal investigations.

Fifth Amendment The U.S. constitutional right guaranteeing that a person will not have to witness against himself in legal proceedings.

hush money Money used to pay people to remain quiet.

impeachment A formal accusation. The United States House of Representatives does not have the power to try or convict government officials accused of crime, but the U.S. Senate does. In order for those accused to be tried in the Senate, however, an impeachment must be first handed down from the House of Representatives.

Operation Gemstone The code name of the Special Investigations Unit's spying operation on the Democratic National Committee.

perjury A lie told in a court of law.

the Plumbers   The seven members of the Special Investigations Unit who performed spying operations for the Committee to Reelect the President.

prosecution   The party accusing the defendant in a court of law.

slush fund   A stash of money used for illegal or secret operations.

Special Investigations Unit   A secret organization within the Committee to Reelect the President. Its mission was to monitor activities considered a threat to the reelection of President Nixon. It is sometimes referred to as the SIU.

subpoena   A legal document that demands that a person or evidence appear before a court of law.

writ of certiorari   A petition to an appellate court to hear a case. If the appellate court agrees to hear a case, it "grants certiorari" to the writ.

Bibliography

Ben-Veniste, Richard, and George Frampton, Jr. *Stonewall: The Real Story of the Watergate Prosecution.* New York: Simon and Schuster, 1977.

Bernstein, Carl, and Bob Woodward. *All the President's Men.* New York: Simon & Schuster, 1974.

Dash, Sam. *Chief Counsel: Inside the Ervin Committee—The Untold Story of Watergate.* New York: Random House, 1976.

Dean, John. *Blind Ambition.* New York: Simon and Schuster, 1976.

Drew, Elizabeth. *Washington Journal: The Events of 1973–1974.* New York: Random House, 1974.

Ehrlichman, John. *Witness to Power.* New York: Simon and Schuster, 1982.

Emery, Fred. *Watergate: The Corruption of American Politics and the Fall of Richard Nixon.* New York: Times Books, 1994.

Friedman, Leo, ed. *United States v. Nixon: The President Before the Supreme Court.* New York: Chelsea House, 1974.

Haldeman, H.R., and Joseph DiMona. *The Ends of Power.* New York: Times Books, 1978.

Hunt, E. Howard. *Undercover: Memoirs of an American Secret Agent.* New York: Berkley, 1974.

Kilpatrick, Carroll. "President Refuses to Turn Over Tapes; Ervin Committee, Cox Issue Subpoenas." *Washington Post* (July 24, 1973): p. A1+.

Kurland, Philip B. *Watergate and the Constitution.* Chicago: The University of Chicago Press, 1978.

Lardner, George. "Cox Is Chosen as Special Prosecutor." *Washington Post* (May 19, 1973): p. A1.

Liddy, G. Gordon. *Will.* New York: St. Martin's, 1980.

Lukas, J. Anthony. *Nightmare: The Underside of the Nixon Years.* New York: Viking, 1976.

Magruder, Jeb Stuart. *An American Life: One Man's Journey to Watergate.* New York: Atheneum, 1974.

Mankiewicz, Frank. *U.S. v. Richard Nixon.* New York: Quadrangle, 1975.

Meyer, Lawrence. "President Taped Talks, Phone Calls." *Washington Post* (July 17, 1973): p. A1+.

Staff of the *New York Times. The End of a Presidency.* New York: Bantam, 1974.

Nixon, Richard M. *RN: The Memoirs of Richard Nixon.* New York: Grosset & Dunlap, 1975.

Schell, Jonathan. *The Time of Illusion.* New York: Knopf, 1976.

Sirica, John J. *To Set the Record Straight: The Break-in, the Tapes, the Conspirators, the Pardon.* New York: Norton, 1979.

Summers, Anthony, and Robbyn Swan. *The Arrogance of Power.* New York: Viking, 2000.

Sussman, Barry. *The Great Cover-up: Nixon and the Scandal of Watergate.* New York: Thomas Y. Crowell, 1974.

U.S. Constitution Online. Available online. URL: www.usconstitution.net. Updated on March 15, 2006.

Further Reading

Feinberg, Barbara S. *Watergate: Scandal in the White House.* London: Franklin Watts, 1990.

Herda, D.J. *U.S. v. Nixon: Watergate and the President.* New York: Enslow, 1996.

Kilian, Pamela. *What Was Watergate?* New York: St. Martin's, 1990.

Web Sites

Watergate Chronology. Washingtonpost.com. Available online. URL: http://www.washingtonpost.com/wp-srv/onpolitics/ watergate/chronology.htm.

Watergate Index. Spartacus Educational. Available online. URL: http://www.spartacus.schoolnet.co.uk/watergate.htm.

Watergate.Info. Available online. URL: http://www.watergate.info/.

Picture Credits

Index

About the Author

Larry A. Van Meter, a native of Phoenix, Arizona, is an English teacher at York College in Nebraska. Before earning his doctorate in English at Texas A&M University, he served in the U.S. Navy as a cryptologist.

Tim McNeese is an associate professor of history at York College, in York, Nebraska. Professor McNeese earned his associate of arts degree from York College, a bachelor of arts in history and political science from Harding University, and a master of arts in history from Southwest Missouri State University. A prolific author of books for elementary, middle, and high school, and college readers, McNeese has published more than 80 books and educational materials over the past 20 years on everything from Mississippi steamboats to Marco Polo. His writing has earned him a citation in the library reference work, *Something About the Author*. In 2005, he published the textbook *Political Revolutions of the 18th, 19th, and 20th Centuries*. Professor McNeese served as a consulting historian for the History Channel program, *Risk Takers, History Makers*. His wife, Beverly, is an assistant professor of English at York College, and they have two children, Noah and Summer, and two grandchildren, Ethan and Adrianna. Readers are encouraged to contact Professor McNeese at tdmcneese@york.edu.